The questions that should be asked at this time are.

1. Are we there yet Dad?
2. Who done it?

Rev 18:4 And I heard another voice out of the heaven saying, Come out of her, my people, that ye have not fellowship in her sins, and that ye do not receive of her plagues:

Author Ray Lyne

Contents

INTRODUCTION

When I was thirty seven I gave my live to the Lord in a remote part of the South West of Western Australia. It was the greatest time of my life because it demonstrated to me God's great power, presence and knowledge and I found that all of the above are without limit.

At that time I was building a house on small rural property and was a driver for Greyhound Coach-lines. Often when I was driving in the night and all was quiet I would listen to the New Testament on a Walkman tape player and for some reason I was always listening to the book of Revelation.

Right from the start I loved Bible prophesy and couldn't get enough of it.

About five years later I attempted to write a book on the subject but it wasn't very good and shelved it; however I never lost interest in the subject and in 2003-2004 I had another attempt and this time I published a book but I was too impetuous and it wasn't in God and so that too was shelved.

Over the past nearly twenty years I have never lost interest in the subject but resigned myself to the fact that it wasn't my call to write a book on End-Times.

From 2005 to 2015 my wife and ran a mission to the Solomon Islands which we ministered to schools. The purpose was to warn the communities that they should not follow our western nations in the in immoral path that we have taken.

For this mission I wrote a book called Western Society in Crisis and distributed it to teachers and pupils which was warmly received.
Since Covid-19 came about and the government locked us up in our homes we stopped going to church because ours closed down. When they reopened segregated services were conducted and so I decided then that we would not participate in that so we started home fellowship meetings.
After some time we decided to do a letter box drop and advertise our group, it was during this time that I would do a fast to see what God wanted to do.
To my surprise while I was having my usual devotional time of prayer and reading Bible prophesies the Lord began to reveal to me the scriptures to me. Sometimes the download was so much I had to write it down immediately.
For thirty five years I have been reading and trying to understand Bible Prophesy and really never fully understood it. Then all of a sudden in a couple of weeks I get more revelation that than what I got in a lifetime.
The second last chapter of the book called “In simple language’ I lay out without all the scriptures and symbols and tell the story of past and what I believe to be the future based on this revelation so people who are not familiar with the Bible prophesy can understand what the contents of this book is.
This is not a prophecy from me but rather what I believe the Bible prophesies are saying about these last days.

My only purpose in doing this work is to glorify God and Jesus for what He did on the cross and I am seeking no reward or status for myself

When I Was A Boy.

I grew up in a small rural town on the Murray River during the nineteen fifties. During those days there were hardly any lawyers offices because people would make deals on a hand shake; your word was your bond and nearly everyone was made to be held accountable by their peers. The difference between then and now is massive and the moral decline is very noticeable for people my age as we have seen both cultures.

- Bread and milk was delivered on horseback.
- Shops closed on Sundays.
- Everyone went to Church.
- Trust, respect, honesty and hard work were the norm.
- Men respected women.
- There was no swearing in front of Ladies.
- Men would give up their seat and open doors for a lady.
- Men who hit a woman was called a coward and made to feel shame.
- Women stayed at home and were day care for their own children.
- There was no divorce.
- The family was the main structure of society, not the government.
- Young girls going on a date would be chaperoned.
- There was no abortion.
- Everyone got married and no one lived out of wedlock.

- Children were educated at school and parenting was left to the parents.
- Young people showed respect to their elders. No one knew what marijuana was.
- It was legal to hold good moral values.
- Homosexuality was a crime.

THE FALL OF MAN.

When Adam and Eve fell in the Garden of Eden they gave their authority to Satan subjected all of humanity to death and eternal separation from God.

Fortunately God had other plans for the people He loved and began setting in place plans to get his people back. This however would be no small task as God Himself was subject to His own laws and degrees that are impossible for Him to break.

Psa 89:34 My covenant will I not break, nor alter the thing that is gone out of my lips.

When God cursed Satan He set into law that Satan was going to lose the battle for mankind but it was going to be a struggle for us. Gen 3:14.

What was to begin from this point is the longest court trial ever to happen. Because Satan was now lord over the kingdoms of this world Matt 4:8-9 and he was also our accuser before God day and night Rev 12:10 & Zech 3:1-2 and all people were now on trial for their eternal salvation.

Just like a court case here on earth when a person is accused of a crime they must appear before a court and face the charges laid against them. The state prosecutes a person and they must prove whether they are innocent or guilty.

During the proceedings the accused has some restrictions, or prison time depending on the severity of the crime.

Only after the court case if they are found to be innocent then they have all restrictions removed.

It is the same for every person born into this world because we are all sinners and fall short of the glory of God Rom 3:23.
This in a fashion makes Satan the state prosecuting council in heaven and it's his job to accuse all people before God while we are alive.
In effect our lives are this perpetual court case and there are only two ways that these proceedings can come to an end.
1. Our death where we face our final judgement.
2. Satan's removal from heaven.
The problem for mankind is that we have committed a capital crime that is punishable by death and our death sentence is to spend eternity in hell and our holding cell while we are on trial is life in our fallen physical bodies that are subject to sickness and death. We must work out our salvation with fear and trembling Phil 2:12 and our only hope for salvation is by grace through Jesus Christ who died for us. However it is at death to our physical body when we get judged to either be acquitted of the pending death sentence and spend eternity in Heaven with Jesus or be condemned to eternal punishment in hell.

THE GREATEST VICTORY

The following are what Jesus achieved when He was raised from the dead and seated next the Father in Heaven.

1. Jesus took the keys to death and Hades Rev 1:18.
2. Reconciliation to God through the shed blood of Jesus.
3. We are healed and delivered by His wounds. Isa 53:5.
4. Through repentance God can forgive our sins and wrong doing, however this is an ongoing process until we die.
5. Allowed Jesus to open the book and break the seven seals that was in God's hand. Interesting that John wept bitterly because he knew the ramification of this book of prophesy not being opened because Bible prophesy would not be fulfilled and that would mean eternity under the dominion of the accuser.

What the cross could not do under Gods law was have Satan removed from being our prosecutor in heaven. This is a right that Satan received at the fall and God could not override his own law.

If it was possible for this to happen then we would be in heaven now and Satan would have been cast out of heaven long ago. It would be impossible for Jesus to receive His bride through the resurrection and rapture because heaven would be legally out of bounds while we are going through court proceedings. In other words we cannot get to heaven while the trial is going for the followings reasons.

1. We haven't been acquitted and that would mean

allowing a possible guilty person to be found innocent.
2. Would be impossible for the wedding to be happening while the court case is happening.
3. It would also be impossible to have the wedding because if Satan is accuser of all the people of the world then that would mean that we would be having the wedding while the generations continue on earth because of Satan's legal right for ongoing lordship over the world from generation to generation literally for all eternity.

ORDER OF PROPHETIC EVENTS

There must be an order of event that takes place because that's the way that God created the universe. A good example of this is that Jesus could not come until the law was revealed through Moses. Otherwise people would not understand God's requirements for life.

The order of events is as follows.

1. The fall of Adam and Eve and the curse of death and separation from God.

2. Noah's flood was the complete and total destruction of all life on earth because all flesh had been contaminated when fallen angels married women and had children by them call the Nephilim Gen 6:4. These where giants and they were not human but were able to bear children through women. This would mean that God's created people were no longer redeemable because of changed DNA and the only spirit in these giants were demon type spirits rather than having the breath of the living God's spirit in them. 3. God's overthrow of Nimrod was an important historical event that was also a covenant event. People were entering into a one world government and God came down in person to put a stop to it. This covenant meant that God would not allow a global government to rule the earth. 4. Abraham was the greatest covenant because he birthed the nation of Israel and is the father of faith for born again Christians. Rom 3:27.

5. The destruction of Sodom was a very critical historical event because its destruction established the covenant that if people were to engage in sexual perversion at a community, or government level then God would intervene personally, Luke 17:28-30. God also came down and visited Sodom in person to try to get their attention but the people were so morally corrupted that it was impossible to reach them. Even when the Angels struck the men with blindness they still tried to get to the door. Gen 19:11.
6. The arrival of Moses established the great and awesome power of God with the deliverance of a whole nation of Israel from under a tyrannical government of Egypt. It was Moses that received the Law from God.
7. Israel's entry into the Promised Land was also an important prophetical event as it set the stage for the nation of Israel to be established where Jesus the savour of the world would be born.
8. Jesus entry was a pivotal point in history because Jesus through His ministry, death and resurrection was the reason why the church was able to be birthed.
9. End-Times would be the next event to take place which is where we are now and this would never been able to happen had Jesus not gone to the cross as we see in Revelation 5:5 because it was only Jesus who could open the book in God's and break the seven seal setting the path for the return of Jesus.
10. Heaven's war and Satan's eviction from heaven would be the next prophetical event to take place as written in Revelation 12:7-9.

11. The taking away of Christians would after the defeat of Satan and him losing the right to accuse people before God, which is known as the rapture. 1 Thess 4:15.

12. The Great Tribulation will follow the rapture; this is also called the time of God's great wrath Rev 16:1-21.

13. Armageddon is the great battle to be fought by Jesus Himself that will end all evil rule on earth,

14. Then finally we enter into 1000 year reign of Jesus in Jerusalem.

All these events have gone in a proper order except the last three or four events and the next event to take place must be the war in heaven where Satan is cast down to the earth.

God must have legal reason or precedent for declaring this war on Satan.

GOD'S MASTER PLAN

When the angels married women in the days of Noah and the DNA of man was altered God completely eradicated them from the earth.

In the days of Lot when God destroyed Sodom and the cities of the plains he completely eradicated all life from those communities.

For Satan that meant he was out of work after the flood because there was no one to accuse or deceive except for Noah and his family.

The same can be said for the cities of the plains because they were no more.

Because Satan had deceived women to marry the angels and all of humanity was polluted then he lost his legal right to accuse the nations of the world because they ceased to exist.

Thus God's master plan was that He made covenant unbeknown to Satan that if he was to ever deceive the nations to change the DNA of people at government level then Satan lost his prosecutorial rights of the human race before the throne of God.

Similar can be said about the Sodom and Gomorrah because Satan had lost the right to accuse those people because they ceased to exist as God sent fire and brimstone down from heaven and destroyed them because of their sexual perversion.

Jesus admitted that if He had sent someone to do miracles in them they would have repented.

Mat 11:23 And as for you, Capernaum! Did you want to lift yourself up to heaven? You will be thrown down to hell! If the miracles which were performed in you had been performed in Sodom, it would still be in existence today!

Seems that God wanted to set a legal precedent that would give Him the right to declare war on Satan and have him removed from heaven if he was to lead the nations to break these two covenants.

The first one was tampering with human DNA and the second is leading the nations of the world to be governed by homosexuals, or homosexual laws.

If this had not happened then the human race would have been a perpetual situation of being under an oppressive evil dictator named Satan.

Sodom could have been saved but there was a bigger picture going on than what Abraham could imagine when he interceded for those cities Gen 18:22-33.

That raises a very interesting question.

"Has Satan been removed from heaven?"

There would be good reason to speculate that this event has now taken place because there is absolutely no doubt that Satan has defiantly broken these two covenants set by God.

Artificial intelligence and trans-humanism can now change what we are thinking and tell us what to think; scientists are able to change our DNA into all sorts of things.

There is plenty of information what has been accomplished over the past 20 years on the internet for everyone to see about these technologies. If we want to look for evidence that Satan is now been cast down to

the earth and in a very bad mood Rev 12:12 then we need to see what is happening around the world.
There is no doubt that the world has entered into a time of deception that has never been seen; also we are on the seeming on the verge of WW3 and facing financial devastation and famine.
However that doesn't prove that Satan has been given the boot out of heaven, and there is no way that anyone can prove that event has taken place because we are flesh and blood and that is a spiritual event.
But judging by what has been happening and what we are heading into it could be safely said that it has, is or is about to taken place.

ECCLESIA

The first time this word is used in the Bible is Matt 16: after Peter makes his confession that Jesus is the Christ from heaven. Jesus then tells Peter that He will build His church (ecclesia) on Peter and this confession. The Strong concordance interprets this word as follows. *ekklēsia ek-klay-see'-ah From a compound of G1537 and a derivative of G2564; a calling out, that is, (concretely) a popular meeting, especially a religious congregation (Jewish synagogue, or Christian community of members on earth or saints in heaven or both): - assembly, church.* This interpretation is not completely correct because Jesus used a Greek word that is about government. If we were there when Jesus spoke to Peter then we would have understood that Jesus was talking about setting up a government, not a church as we know it. Ecclesia in the time that Jesus said that word meant a place of meeting where everyone is welcome to come and conduct government business such as declaring wars, appointing judges and other community projects. If Jesus was talking about setting up a church as we practice today then He would have used the word Synagogue because it is also a Greek word that was used in the time of Jesus. Below is the Strong's Concordance for the interpretation of the word Synagogue *συναγωγή sunagōgēsoon-ag-o-gay' From (the reduplicated form of) G4863; an assemblage of persons; specifically a Jewish "synagogue" (the meeting or the place); by analogy a Christian church: - assembly, congregation, synagogue.* This church or ecclesia that

Jesus wants to set has nothing to do with worldly governments. It is a completely separate entity. Just because we are to be separate body of people from a worldly government doesn't mean that we don't have anything to do with what happens in the town square debate.

To believe the lie that we are only a mission into the world and so therefore we should stay out of politics really advances the cause of Satan's kingdom. Proof of this is how Jesus interacted with the ruling class of His time. In Matthew 23 Jesus really got into the politicians of the day by calling out publically the moral decadence of the leaders. Some may argue that Israel was a different political system and was under the rule of Rome.

However by the very fact that Christians have a set of laws that we must adhere to is evidence of our political status. Also, as some argue that we are a mission into the world, which we are, then this is even more evidence of our political standing because we are trying to influence people to follow God's law. This is because the very mission that we are doing is telling people they must repent and follow a set of laws that will in most cases run contrary to the worldly political powers. The trend to withdraw from the town square has really been more prominent since WW2. It's not too difficult to see the effect of this withdrawal as the great falling away we have witnessed has happened because of this silence. The education for the masses was initiated and started by the church and now we see that not only has this been taken away from the church but Satan kingdom is extremely well entrenched there shutting the door on any Christian input. Satan has been greatly successful against the church by making the church come under his authority and keeping her silent. It is no wonder that we see so few miracles and moving of the Holy Spirit in today's churches. Communist countries around the world see this very clearly, they understand that the church is an opposition political party that is trying to persuade people to follow God's law. As western nations around the world move further away from God and become more and more immoral they too see that the church is a threat to their agenda and are now busy making and passing laws to silence and shut down the church.

UNHOLY ALLIANCE

Is Tax free really free?

Most churches in Australia signup to become a tax free entity. This was adopted into to our government when we became a nation in 1901 as it was in England for hundreds of years. This was in effect a follow on from England.

However when we became a nation the 10 commandments were built into our constitution, but since then successive governments have overturned all of these Godly laws.

This is the main reason why churches have to go through a rather rigorous process to become tax free now.

It is required that churches follow a strict set of rules and sign an agreement or contract to gain this status. The first step is to become incorporated and to do this the church must set up a governing board and membership of people who attend.

This is done through the state governments and there are many rules and legalities that churches must adhere to.

Example: Churches are subject to audits and must comply because if they don't then an inspector is appointed and can force leaders to do so with the use of police if necessary.

In other words the government can send men with guns into your church and shoot and kill whoever resists these rules. Once the church has established its incorporation status it must apply for tax free status

with a state government department. In Victoria it is the Department of Consumer Affairs.
Once this has been approved the church then applies for tax free status with the ATO (Australian Tax Office). One of the conditions for exemption is that the church must not speak against a political party or candidate. The tax Free Church in Australia today must hand complete authority over to the state government and after that then the federal government prevents church leaders from calling out immoral politicians or policies.

COVENANT

When I trained to be a prison officer the very first thing that we were taught that the operating procedures were what was called the Bible for the prison and it was to be followed to the letter or else we would face dismissal or prison.

Not long after starting I very quickly understood why management drummed that into us.

The problem is that prisons are full of criminals who don't stop being criminals just because they go to jail. That requires a set of laws that govern them from the time they get up until they go to sleep. That's exactly how prison is; they stand to attention next to their bed or cell door for wake up count then after that there is breakfast count, followed by work count where they muster in their compounds.

That's just gets them to work and then there are counts for all other events. They are restricted to their own units and aren't allowed to visit other units unless they get special permission. Even their phone calls and contacts are vetted and monitored.

This is absolute covenant living and if the slightest violation of any prison operating procedures are broken then appropriate penalties are applied.

Christianity is a system of laws which are the ten-commandments that must be obeyed and the effects of disobedience could be as simple as mood change or losing one's salvation. The problem is that these laws have a spiritual effect and aren't always as obvious as those broken in prison. God word tells us not to make covenant with evil governments and when churches signup for tax-free or any other program then they are breaking covenant and therefore not allowing Christ to be fully operational in His own church.

Safe Church Program

Just to make sure that they have control over the congregation as well they make them follow a government mandate by doing an OH&S course.

Since the royal commission into institutions child sexual abuse churches are now required to run an accredited so called Safe Church program for all leadership.

The purpose of this program is meant to protect children from sexual predators.

This may sound like a great idea in theory, but it is a disastrous for the Church of Jesus Christ.

The course makes all men look really bad and not to be trusted by the very fact of doing a course to be on the lookout for a possible sex offender.

Most child molesters are men and churches have been a safe haven for these criminals to access victims in the past.

However this is a completely ineffective way of dealing this problem for two reasons.

1. Sex offenders are extremely deceptive and even if a church was to run a weekly safe church session it would not be successful in uncovering an offender. 1 Cor 12:7-11 The Holy Spirit is far better to protect against this problem with the nine fold spiritual gifts that have been given to the church for this very purpose.

2. Australian governments both federal and state have become so evil and corrupt that to bow the knee in obedience to this is pushing the Holy Spirit out of the church. Amazing hypocrisy by a government that funds and supports the sexual abuse of children through its education departments to tell the church what is moral and right. What's even more unbelievable is that the church has swallowed this rubbish and followed in lockstep.

I worked as a prison office in a protection prison for eleven years and spend eighteen months working in a protection unit especially for child sex offenders. It was an eye opener to how these people operate and think. The first thing that was very noticeable about these men was they were very friendly and did all they could to get you to like them. At the beginning that seemed like a good thing because there were not many behaviour management problems and so from a prison officer perspective that seemed a good deal.

However after some time working with these men I began to realise that they were masters of manipulation, deception and wanting to control all and everyone around them.

I found that after the eighteen months with these men I really had a difficult time working in that unit because the manipulation and lack of victim empathy and so went and worked with the mainstream offenders. Jesus said that it would be better to have a millstone around the neck and thrown into the sea than offend one of these little ones. Luke 17:2.

There are many individual cases that I could quote about this problem but for the purpose of space I will give one really interesting example so you can grasp of the level of deception of these men who offend against children.

Robert Lowe murdered Sheree Beasley on 29th June 1991 in Frankston Victoria Sheree was only six years old at the time. Lowe had kidnapped, raped and murdered Sheree and then disposed of her body in a stormwater drain.

Lowe was employed as a salesman and was a member of the Brighton Uniting Church who was very well respected by all. He had a wife and two sons who wholly supported him throughout the murder trial.

Lowe had always maintained that he was innocent and kept a huge amount material in his cell that he was constantly working on to be acquitted of the crime that he emphatically claimed he did not do.

Lowe came across as a very polite well-mannered man who would never get flustered while in prison. That would be difficult for anyone because of the cramped condition and the continual meal queues and muster counts.

After some time of observing Lowe and his behaviour I started to wonder if he was wrongly convicted and so I decided to read his court and trial proceedings. The best way to describe the difference of the man and the evidence in court and his daily interaction and behaviour is he is a true doctor Jekyll and Mr Hyde.

This man was so evil and a master manipulator that even his philologist turned states witness against him because of the mind games he was playing on her. Even the police who investigated and had all the evidence against him said that they had never seen one so deceptive.

Yet at the same time to church community and work peers he was a shining citizen who anyone would trust. Lowe did have a history of prior arrests however he was usually able to talk his way out of a conviction.

What I realised that if I had met Lowe at a church that I too would have trusted him completely and could even be a friend to him.

If church leaders knew the level of deceptive behaviour that these men will go to be accepted and trusted they would realise that there is not a Safe Church Program on the planet that would stop them. The truth of it is a child sex offender would see the program a challenge for them to overcome and consider it a game.

CENTRELINK

Another government contract that churches enter is with Centrelink; these are so the church can gain financial help from the federal government for doing some form of outreach into the community.

This may be an employment program for the unemployed, or something of this nature. In order for a church to sign up with Centrelink once again there is a host of rules and regulations that the church must adhere to, again abdicating authority away from Jesus and giving it to the king of Sodom.

Even though it may appear on the surface that the church is an independent and sovereign entity; 'That really is very far from the truth as has been pointed out!

I guess the real issue here is what does God's Word say about this situation?

First thing to consider is what type of federal and state governments do we have in Australia today, and what are their moral stances?

Every state in Australia fund late term abortion. Even babies who have been born alive can be murdered if the mother changes her mind and doesn't want the child.

Euthanasia is now allowed for people wanting to end their lives early, which is murder.

Every state in Australia teach some form of the Safe School program which really is the sexualisation and homosexualization of children on mass. The sexualisation of children was what caused God to come and personally visit Sodom and Gomorrah, Gen chapters 19. The worst part of that is that the people of those

cities were so demented and perverted that they missed their visitation from God.
Pornography and prostitution both legalized.
Our government are just about a mirror image of Sodom and Gomorrah and our churches are lining up to sign up for a cash bonus of not having to pay tax.
Jesus said in Matthew 22:15-22 give to Caesar what Caesar's and give to God what is God's.
Put more simply:
'Pay your taxes church!
Abraham said to the king of Sodom after he helped free him from captivity and Sodom's ruler wanted to reward Abraham for his help by giving him some reward.
Gen 14:21 The king of Sodom said to Abram, "Keep the loot, but give me back all my people."
Gen14:22 Abram answered, "I solemnly swear before the LORD, the Most High God, Maker of heaven and earth, 14:23 that I will not keep anything of yours, not even a thread or a sandal strap. Then you can never say, 'I am the one who made Abram rich.'
Isaiah the prophet also calls this dependency on ungodly governments for protection and help as a sin that will lead to disaster.
Isa 30:1 *The LORD has spoken: "Those who rule Judah are doomed because they rebel against me. They follow plans that I did not make, and sign treaties against my will, piling one sin on another. 30:2 They go to Egypt for help without asking for my advice. They want Egypt to protect them, so they put their trust in Egypt's king. 30:3*

But the king will be powerless to help them, and Egypt's protection will end in disaster.
Isaiah 31:1 *Those who go to Egypt for help are doomed! They are relying on Egypt's vast military strength—horses, chariots, and soldiers. But they do not rely on the LORD, the holy God of Israel, or ask him for help. 31:2 He knows what he is doing! He sends disaster. He carries out his threats to punish evil people and those who protect them. 31:3 The Egyptians are not gods—they are only human. Their horses are not supernatural. When the LORD acts, the strong nation will crumble, and the weak nation it helped will fall. Both of them will be destroyed* Moses commanded the Israelites as part of the law not to enter into covenants with evil nation. *Exo 23:32 You shall make no covenant with them or with their gods.*
For ten years I ran a part-time mission to the Solomon Islands and when I started I basically had nothing. My dining set was a foldup card table and two folding chairs, the lounge was a deck chair and I had an old 18inch portable TV. I paid $20.00 for an old bed out of a motel that was closing down and my car was old beat up 1976 Toyota.
Had very little money in the bank and was renting a cheap flat in the poor side of town. Then the Lord called me to go to the Solomon Islands. I managed to scrape up enough for the air fares and spending money and we went on our first mission in 2006. By the time my wife and I had finish our last trip in 2015 we had a new home

paid for, plus nearly new car, furniture and a good healthy savings account.

What I learnt was it is really exciting let God supply our needs especially when you are doing His work. If the church was to do the same it would witness the power of God to provide for His church and I know that that really does thrill God to do that. The church can legally operate as a group of people that meet and do not have to go through binding covenants. As far as I am concerned when a group of believers meet to worship God and have fellowship it has absolutely nothing to do with these evil governments. The churches only government should Jesus under the power of the Holy Spirit and completely separate from our government as the scriptures clearly point out.

THE WORK OF THE CROSS

The work of the cross wasn't finished two thousand years ago at Jerusalem because it was only the beginning of the war that was and still is being waged against Satan.

The Cross was a pivotal moment in this war like the battle of Midway 4th June 1942 was in WW2 when the American navy defeated the Japanese through better intelligence even though the Japanese had a stronger navy. WW2 didn't end at Midway, but rather went for another three years and two months with many more terrible battles to be fought with millions more being killed.

The great victory that Jesus had on the cross was He took the keys to Death & Hades and Jesus became the first fruits of the resurrection preparing the way for the seventh trumpet blast of God and the resurrection of the dead and the rapture.

What Jesus achieved was by taking the key from Satan He was able to take charge of those who were in paradise. It says in Ephesians four and eight that the when Jesus ascended up into heaven that He led captivity captive. Because He died for us and His innocent blood was shed for our wrong doing death was unable to hold Him in Paradise and unable to keep Paradise under Satan's control.

Paradise was under the earth where the saints were kept as we see from the situation of the rich man in hell and Lazarus the beggar in the bosom of Abraham Luke 16:19-34. Also when Jesus was on the cross and the thief asked Jesus to remember him, and Jesus said today you will be in Paradise with me Luke 23:43. Jesus went down into the earth for three days and then He rose from the dead; He never went to Heaven until He had risen.

It is unclear exactly what the spiritual situation of those that Jesus released from under the earth but we have to assume that it was much better than before.

Paul does say in 1 Cor 15:51 that we will not all sleep and so we have to assume that is the situation.

The release of paradise was the catalyst for the birthing of the Church because up until then there was no pathway to heaven for people because they were under the legal jurisdiction of Satan because of the fall.

This unbelievable act of heroism by Jesus was the start of the Church here on earth because we now from this point had a clear pathway to heaven. This is why it says in the very same verse that He gave gifts to men and those gifts were Apostle, Prophet, Evangelist, Teacher and Pastor.

God through Moses and Israel set up the Law that God required men to live by and obey in order that they could access heaven and be set free from Satan's control. In other words God did make a path for salvation through Israel that if we obeyed the Law then we get to go to heaven.

However no one was able to obey the Law during their lifetime and so Satan had control of those in paradise to be kept in a state of sleep down under the earth. Then Jesus through His perfect sinless life made it possible for

us to go to heaven so long as we repent from our sins and accept Jesus Christ as our Lord and saviour.
This act set the stage here on earth for a second kingdom and that is the church. This second kingdom is contrary and in opposition to the earthly one that Satan controls and that's the very reason from the beginning of the Church in Jerusalem saints were brutally treated. The church in effect was started with the mandate to wage war against the governments of the world. However the war is different to the way that the government.
Paul tells us in 2 Cor 10:4 that the weapons of our warfare are not physical but spiritual and that it is fought in the realm of the spirit. However in order to fight such a spiritual war it takes some physical action or words to do that and we usually call that an act of faith. We see that the disciples did that when they defied the orders of the rulers of Jerusalem when they were told not to mention the name of Jesus by the governing rulers, they said we must obey God rather than man. Compare that to the pastors today who obeyed the government to defy Gods commandment to not forsake the fellowship Heb 10:25. Note that it says that we are to do this so much more when we see the day approaching of the Lords return.
Jesus set Paradise free because of the cross.
Jesus birthed the Church because of the cross. Jesus gave the fivefold ministry gifts to set the captives free here from the bond of Satan.

The church that does not promote, teach and develop these gifts allows believers to be still in bondage to Satan.

The situation here on earth is a two thousand year stalemate of two armies, one being the demonic strongholds led by Satan and the church led by Jesus Christ with the empowerment of the Holy Spirit.

What God needed was a legal loophole to catch Satan out so that there may be a shift in this spiritual war and that came about by Satan over playing his hand by his earthly governments developing laws that would turn the next generation into Sodomites and change human DNA.

There are two governments in heaven; God's Government is in the highest heaven and Satan's government is in the second heaven. Same as we have two governments here on earth, Satan's is the worldly governments and God's is the Church or a better word would Ecclesia, which really means government and not church.

The next major battle to be fought and won will be Revelation twelve where Satan is cast out of heaven and loses to the right to be accuser before God and this battle could never be fought had Jesus not given His life at Calvary and thus we see just how important that the Church never dismiss or treat the message of the cross lightly. Unfortunately we do see this happen in many churches today because of the way the communion is treated as many churches only have communion twice a month. This usually goes with that statement:

"I have moved past the cross!"
I am not sure where there is to move to considering that we are healed by the cuts on Jesus back where His blood flowed from and it by that shed blood that we are forgiven.
That is healing, deliverance and forgiveness of sins; 'what more is there?
Isa 53:5 But He was wounded for our transgressions, He was bruised for our iniquities; The chastisement for our peace was upon Him, And by His stripes we are healed.
Satan is the tempter and accuser while Jesus forgives and corrects.

MARXISM

An example of just how far we have strayed from a Christian based democracy is demonstrated in Victoria Australia under the leadership of Premier Daniel Andrews who was elected in 2014.

The policies that he has implemented are extreme and an all-out attack on the Church and Christians. Andrews has used the Gay Lobby as his tool for destroying our Christian democracy and heritage.

An example of just how influential and powerful the Gay Lobby has become is what happened in Sate Parliament when Daniel Andrews made his apology to the gay community on 23rd May 2016. The following is an extract from his famous speech to the Victorian Parliament and community when a rainbow flag was flown over Parliament House in Melbourne.

Mr Andrews demonstrated a great deal of passion and commitment to turning the situation around. The bracketed inserts are my comments. Mr Andrews states, 'we are building a society that is strong and just and in doing so speaker we will have shown this moment to be no gesture..................

1. (The warning to the Christian community) There was a time in history when we turned thousands of ordinary young men into criminals................ This was profoundly and unimaginably wrong.................... The law required them (Government) to be bigoted....... One of those laws was even labelled as an abomination............

2. (The denouncing of the Word of God Lev 18:22 and turning God fearing Christians into criminals for

speaking the truth......"Hate speech") We can't conceive what was on the minds of our forbearers in this place (Parliament)................

3. (He knew exactly what and why these laws were established. Our Christian heritage.) There is so much more we need to do to make things right............................

4. (Further warning to the Christian community) You have a Government and Parliament that is on your side (To the LGBT community).

5. (The Government is at war with Christians as he has declared here) You have a Government that is trying to make the state a safer place in the school and workplace.

6. (The new sex-education from pre-schoolers up for complete moral breakdown and brainwashing of the next generation.) You have a Government that trying to eradicate a culture of bullying so the next generation will not have to experience it.

7. (Government is out to eradicate Bible believing Christians) All Christians should be extremely concerned about this because the State Labor Government has made a public declaration of war against the true Church. The reason why there were laws outlawing homosexuality was because of the Leviticus Law and the 10 Commandments that our nation and constitution was established on. Mr Andrews cleverly makes no mention of this fact in his speech but he is very well aware of it. You must realize that these modern days

Marxists are extremely clever and professional about how they will conduct this war.
The tactics they employ mostly go unnoticed by the Christian community. Back in the bad old days of Marxist Communism the leaders would simply kill or imprison anyone who resisted their tyranny. During the Cold War they tried to defeat the west through military means but found that this would be counterproductive because it would cause global destruction.
These modern day Marxists have gained and continue to gain power by stealth with the education system, media, social media, Hollywood, Liberal Churches and other institutions. They use terms like, 'inclusive, love, modernism, progressive and accepting of all. This bears witness when listening to what Daniel Andrews said in his speech above.
To the average Christian it seems to be not too threatening but when you listen to what he is saying and then look at the changes the government has made and want to make in less than 2 years of coming to power it becomes very clear the Church is at war with the Government of Victoria.
1. This government has banned religious lessons for schools.
2. Put a 100 meter no-go zone for Christian protestors and counsellors around abortion clinics.
3. Implemented the immoral sex-education program from pre-schoolers and up.
4. They are in the process of making it illegal for

Christian schools and Churches to employ people only of the same faith.

This declaration of war is centred on the Bible verse in Leviticus. Lev 18:22 Thou shalt not lie with man, as with woman: it is abomination.

Mr Andrews even quotes the word abomination in his speech, but without reference to the Bible demonstrating just how clever and non-confrontational he is in changing laws and getting little reaction from the Christian community.

The Premier said in his speech to the LGBT community, 'we are on your side! What he is really saying to the true church is that we are coming after you because we have changed sides. The government has the time and the resources to wage and win this war as can be seen by what has happened to our community and Church since WW2.

SIN OF MANASSEH

It's very possible that we have reached what is called the 'Sin of Manasseh'.

Since the election of Daniel Andrews he has not only done all in his power to remove our Christian heritage but has replaced it with some of the most evil and ungodly laws imaginable.

The new conversion therapy law is in effect the criminalisation of the faith.

The very fact that we are no longer allowed under state law to minister to a homosexual for them to be able to repent from that life style is the outlawing of the Christian faith.

As the *Victorian Animal Part MP Andy Meddick put it. He does not believe the legislation will stop religious ministers explaining the teaching of their faith. "What it will stop them from doing is berating that person telling them there is something wrong with them and from going down a path to correct them,"*

That is an oxymoron because the whole purpose of Christianity is to call to people to repent from their sins and follow Jesus Christ in order to avoid eternity in hell and transgenderism and homosexuality is a sin that needs to be repented of to receive that salvation.

This is what the Bible teaches and there is no amount of theological gymnastics that can change that fact.

Daniel Andrews has led us on a path that there may be no return just the same as Manasseh did with Judah.

2Ki 24:2 The LORD sent armed bands of Babylonians, Syrians, Moabites, and Ammonites against Jehoiakim to destroy Judah, as the LORD had said through his servants the prophets that he would do. 24:3 This happened at the LORD's command, in order to banish the people of Judah from his sight because of all the ***sins that King Manasseh had committed,***

Manasseh crimes were child sacrifice which Daniel Andrews has done by legislating late term abortion which means killing babies alive after birth; he even voted against allowing doctors to give the infant some pain killer during the murder.

Our premier and many other state premiers and governors have been possessed by the spirit of Manasseh.

2 Kings 21:3 says that Manasseh followed Ahab the wicked king of Israel whose wife was Jezebel and they had done worse than what the nations did that they overthrew to occupy the land. Their sins were as bad as Sodom and Gomorrah we see that we have returned to the days of Sodom because of the all-powerful Marxist Gay Political Lobby and Daniel Andrews has been the mover and shaker of that.

Since Andrews has made all these evil laws we have experienced one curse after the next with the worst bushfires and drought in our history and now we have the plague of Covid-19 and the next curse that will strike the land will be a depression of the likes we have never seen before which will cause a famine.

Lev 26:19 And I will break the pride of your power, and I will make your heaven like iron and your earth like bronze.

1Sa 4:8 Woe to us! Who shall deliver us out of the hand of these mighty gods? These are the gods that struck the Egyptians with all the plagues in the wilderness.
These are wicked and evil people that will lead their constituents down a road of death and destruction just as they have legislated.

DECEPTION

The main characteristic of the End-Times will be deception as it was the first point that Jesus raised when he prophesied what was to take place in 70AD with the destruction of Jerusalem and the scattering of the Jews; also the foretelling of events in the very last days when the Antichrist would be revealed. Matt 24:4. Clearly deception was extremely prevalent in the days of Jesus and the Apostles. Jesus and the Apostles did the most amazing miracles and signs. The dead were raised, the sick healed, the lame walked and many were delivered from demonic possession and oppression and miracles of every type and yet the ruling class rather than celebrating this were jealous.

This was the response from the community leaders in a time that there was no medical help for these poor people who were suffering from their ailments.

This demonstrates their hardness and that they were prepared to go to any lengths to be seen as the most pious and right standing in the community.

Even after Jesus raised Lazarus from the dead the only thing these evil men could see was losing their place in the community. It was then that they decided to have Jesus killed. It seems almost inconceivable that they would look at the situation like that, even after they had witnessed someone who had the power over life and death.

That led to the greatest single act of deception of all time when Judas betrayed Jesus for thirty pieces of silver. Today we are entering into a time of great deception; however the deception that is sweeping the whole world now covers nearly every aspect of life, these include scientific biology, politics, judicial, education, media, entertainment, Covid-19, economy and religion.

ANCIENT GOVERNMENTS AND BUREAUCRACIES

Not until the twentieth century did governments or kingdoms become so large with many different bureaucracies that service the community in nearly every aspect of life.

Earlier kingdoms raised taxes for military, law and justice, their own lavish lifestyles and some other projects like constructing roads and maybe water ducts as the ancient Romans did.

In general the population had to fend for itself with health, education and other community services. Kings and lords were generally only interested in their own situations and making sure the serfs paid their taxes.

MORDERN GOVERNMENT

In this modern political world we see that government bureaucracies control nearly all aspects of life.

1. Law and Justice.
2. Technology science.
3. Religion
4. Education.
5. Sexuality.
6. Climate.
7. Media.
8. Entertainment.
9. Business and Finance.
10. Health.

All of the above been are either run by government bureaucracies, or have government support which means that there are rules attached to receive funds.

Religion is supported by government via tax free status that most churches adopt so they don't have to pay tax. But in order to receive that the government gains a huge amount of control.

Entertainment is generally independent but has huge sway over the population because movies are often a statement being made about current political and social events. In Australia our state governments have bureaucratic departments that produce movies and TV series as do many communist countries.

Media outlets are run by a handful of huge companies but again here in Australia we have a state run news outlet called the Australian Broadcasting Company which is Marxist and spews out communist propaganda very similar to what Chinese and North Korean media outlets do.

Everyone one of these bureaucracies have become so evil, corrupt and deceitful in the last twenty years that it's got to the point that they can't get much worse. Everyone one of these entities now promotes same sex marriage and children being brainwashed about what gender identity they are.

There isn't any place to go from here; this is without question the greatest deception that society has accepted. Twenty years ago if you said this is what community leaders were advocating people would say that you were insane to believe such stupidity.

The interesting part of this is that we see that there are ten bureaucracies that have become part of the United Nations and many world governments. They are independent and connected to government as they control different aspects of day to day life and yet are funded by government.

For instance the health department has its own power as we found out during the Covid-19 pandemic because the premiers and state governors were under the control of the head health officers. This same principal applies to all the government bureaucracies because elected politicians can't override what these departments do.

THE BEAST

The beast that rises out of the sea in Revelation 13:1 has seven heads and ten horns and so the first question to ask is what is the beast and when does it appear.

The Bible tells us that the beast is a political system or kingdom, because when Satan tempted Jesus he showed him all the worlds' kingdoms and governments of the world and offered them to Jesus if was to bow down and worship him Matt 4:9. Also Satan is described in Revelation twelve as having seven heads and ten horns same as the beast.

This beast doesn't appear until the very last three and half years before the return of the Lord.

Rev 13:5 And there was given unto him a mouth speaking great things and blasphemies; and power was given unto him to continue forty and two months.

This End-Time beast has ten horns with crowns on indicating that this government will have ten micro governments that are connected to it. Revelation 17:12 tells us that these kingdoms will have power for a little while then they will hand that power to the beast.

Maybe a better way to describe this is that these micro kingdoms emerge from the main political system then they hand it back after a short time.

If we are on the verge of the return of the Lord then there should be some evidence of these emerging powers.

Political powers don't just appear out of thin air as they take many years to evolve to the point of leadership.

A couple of very good examples of this fact is the summit of Nazi and Soviet power.
Hitler joined the Nationalist movement and attempted a coup in November 1923 which failed and then Hitler never came to power in 1933.
In 1905 the communists attempted a coup and also failed, it wasn't until November of 1917 that they succeeded in overthrowing the Czar.
If these micro kingdoms or bureaucracies are the ten horns on the beast there needs to be a closer examination of them and their conduct, in particular deception as this is Satan's greatest weapon.
The escalation of deception in politics has been like a tsunami in just the last ten years. With the victory of Donald Trump in 2016 he exposed for all to see the level of corruption, deception and dishonesty in the political establishment.
However it really escalated in November 2020 when the USA election was held.
Biden did not win that election it was a coup, it was a complete fraud for all to see. In the swing states when it was evident that Trump was going to romp in they stopped the public count and continued in secret.
From that point on Donald Trump never got another vote. Also disclosed film footage of democrats rolling out suitcases full of votes; Republican observers refused entry into the counting rooms to keep an eye on any possibility of cheating.
Both social and mainstream were media behind the coup and refusing to expose the criminal fraud that the

democrats were doing and going as far to call anyone who questioned what happened as divisive and a potential right wing terrorist.

The murder of Seth Rich on the 10/07/2016 when he was shot and murdered in Washington DC Seth worked for the Democratic Party as a computer man and was sending information to Julian Assange's Wikileaks information about Clinton's criminal ties to Russia just before the 2016 election in which Donald Trump won. When Seth was murdered the police would not disclose much information, and the motive for the murder was not robbery as nothing was taken. It is believed that it was a hit because of his leaking of information that would damage Hilary Clinton chances of winning the 2016 election against Donald trump.

Insurrection Day 9th January 2021 when protesters storm Capitol Hill in Washington that it is now famously called.

The establishment want everyone to believe that this was the worst crime to ever happen in America; even worse than the civil war. They would have gotten away with this fraud except that so many of the protestors had their own cameras and the world was able to see what really happened.

Antifa were responsible for the break in and were sent for that purpose so that it looked like the people who were supporting Donald Trump would be blamed. The police must have been in on the break in as well as they did nothing to stop the protestors from getting in. Keep in mind that it was their job to protect the politicians who were in the building at the time. These police are there to do all they can to protect the government and it is plain for all to see that they were told to stand down.

Many of the people who got access into the building were arrested for trespass and are still in solitary confinement in prison. Then compare that to Black Lives Matter who were responsible for burning and looting countless American cities. Those who were caught in the act of terrorism were immediately bailed and returned to their lawless acts. Black Lives Matter who are allied the Democratic party in America are supposed to be for the support of non-whites worldwide.

When they rose to proneness after the death of George Floyd 25th May 2020 when he died of a drug overdose; not murder, BLM web page stated on the About Us page that they were committed Marxists that were dedicated to the destruction of both the nucleus family and Christian based democracy. Since they have become popular globally they have deleted that from their web page.

Conservative white men who are Christian and nationalistic (love their country) are now considered by the FBI as being as dangerous as the Taliban. FBI director Wray at a House Homeland Security Committee Hearing on the 17th November 2020 confirmed this when asked at the hearing.

CSIS The Centre for Strategic and International Studies is a think tank based in Washington, D.C. They are a major influence in US politics and state that white males who

are Christian and are anti-abortionists are as dangerous as Al-Qaida.
It is becoming the norm when listening to the media or politicians for them to keep on spewing this shameless propaganda and this is not confined to the USA only but every western country around the world.
The murder of Ashli Babbitt on the 8th January 2021by a Capitol Hill police officer. The name of the officer has never been disclosed and after seeing the footage it almost looks like it was a deliberate hit on this poor woman. The officer seemed to take his time and stepped out into the hallway to get a better a look, or aim at the victim. At the time of the shooting Ashli wasn't doing anything wrong, she was standing up on a window ledge while other protestors were smashing the doors in and were allegedly Antifa who were extremely violent, the shooter took his time to take the shot. It wasn't a random wild shot.
This is out there for everyone to see yet nothing is either said or done about this.
The Democrat's want to hold a 9/11 type enquiry into the breaking in of Capitol Hill so they can further label white Christian conservatives as would be terrorist and a danger to the nation. This is no different to Daniel Andrews so call Conversion Therapy law that he has recently passed. Christians are now the enemy of the state and the government is coming after us and nothing will stop them.

LAW AND JUSTICE

The Victorian government have passed a law which prevents parents, doctors, councillors and clergy from trying to talk a child from having a sex change. The penalty is up to ten years jail.

In other words parents send their children to school to be brainwashed by activist teachers to have a sex change and there is nothing the parent can do except obey.

This law is the greatest deception that has ever been adopted by a legal system anywhere in the world history.

The statue that represents the justice department in western countries is a blindfolded lady who has a pair of scales in her hand. The scales are for equal justice for all under the law and the blindfold means impartiality.

Under left-wing Marxist governments that have now nearly taken over western democracies we see that the scales have become weighed down heavily to the left and the blindfold has been ripped off.

In December 2018 Cardinal George Pell was found guilty of child sexual abuse and awaited sentencing in Victoria. However on appeal to the Australian High Court Pell was acquitted of all charges.

George Pell never had any history of child sexual abuse, or any suspicion of such conduct.

It was alleged that he just randomly sexually assaulted a choir boy directly after mass in the change room before his traditional meeting of the people after the service.

There was hardly any time for him to get changed let alone sexually abuse someone on the way.
Yet he was found guilty of the offence. There was only one allegation against him; however the ABC (Australian Broadcasting Company) a dedicated left-wing Marxist media outlet had him convicted before the verdict was even reached.
Also Daniel Andrews was premier of Victoria at that time and had stacked the justice department with Marxist activist judges.
Cardinal Pell at the time of his trial was about to expose some very serious corruption at the highest level of the Vatican. It was said that millions of dollars had gone missing and Pell was going to reveal it. The people who Pell was going after had sent money to the Victorian Government to help in the conviction.
Roger Stone a very close friend to President Donald Trump had his home raided and was arrested by the FBI for allegedly giving false information to congress on the 26th January 2019. Stone whose wife has some medical issues and Roger who is 68 years old never would be any threat what so ever to arresting officers, yet at least twelve heavily armed men dressed in SWAT gear took part in the raid.
CNN a Marxist left-wing media outlet based in the USA was tipped off about the raid and covered it to make Stone look like some kind of really bad criminal.
The Justice department in the US decided to empty prisons as a means of reducing Coved-19 infections. They allowed violent criminals into the community and

the crime statistics have gone through the roof since doing that.

Many leftists don't believe in prison as they say that there is no evil in the world, just misguided people who are less fortunate than others. They implement all sorts of program's that are offence related.

These are a dismal failure and the evidence of this is the ESO (Extended Supervision Orders). These are for sex offenders who are deemed to be too dangerous to allow back into the community and are sent to special accommodation units where they are not allowed into the community unless they are supervised, or escorted. All these offenders have done the sex offender program while they were incarcerated but have failed to respond to treatment. Jesus said it would be better to have a millstone put around the neck than offend one of these little ones Matt 18:6.

Nearly all inmates attend these programs because if they refuse then parole is revoked and they must serve their full sentence. This is why many have a rather long parole period which serves a carrot or incentive to participate in the program even if they are not genuine. The justice department reduce their recidivism rate by not counting a reoffender if five years have lapsed without being successfully prosecuted. This is what is called cooking the books.

Since most governments around the world have become Marxist they have politicized their police forces. No longer are the police employed to serve and protect; instead they have become foot soldiers for these left-wing socialist governments. Evidence of this has been the massive overreach of power worldwide since the Covid-19 pandemic.

Citizens who have opposed these lockdowns and tried to protest have been brutally treated by police while at the same time when there has been a BLM protests they have been given a free pass, and often encouraged by both government and media.

Seems as though the justice department have become as deceptive and dishonest as the real criminals they have sent to prison.

There is no question that our current legal system would qualify to be a horn on this Antichrist beast.

TECHNOLOGY SCIENCE

Science is just about completely run by government and it is in the name of medical science doctors are mutilating children with sex change surgery and experimental drugs to block puberty.

It was the head medical advisors that caused the shutdowns, made everyone wear a mask and demanded everyone get vaccinated or lose everything.

With technology giants Facebook, Twitter and YouTube doing their bidding for them by censoring anyone who challenged the narrative. Debate wasn't allowed and sadly most of the population was in lockstep with their lies and propaganda.

The technology is now available to have a microchip planted in the human brain and control a person's thoughts and read their minds. This technology is what the Bible calls the mark of the beast 666 Revelation 13:16-18.

Technology has open the world up to an evil of a dimension that has never happened and that is the easy availability of pornography. It is one of the largest and wealthiest online industries there is. Children have easy access to it which is extremely harmful to the young developing mind. It completely corrupts the relationship between a man and a woman and it is any wonder that young people avoid marriage.

Pornography is a destructive tool that the Satan is using to prepare the world for the arrival of the Antichrist.

The state of mind of people who engage in pornography regularly puts them in a extremely dangerous situation which is best described in the following scripture.

Rom 1:18 For the wrath of God is revealed from heaven against all ungodliness and unrighteousness of men, who hold the truth in unrighteousness; 19 Because that which may be known of God is manifest in them; for God hath shewed it unto them. 20 For the invisible things of him from the creation of the world are clearly seen, being understood by the things that are made, even his eternal power and Godhead; so that they are without excuse: 21 Because that, when they knew God, they glorified him not as God, neither were thankful; but became vain in their imaginations, and their foolish heart was darkened. 22 Professing themselves to be wise, they became fools, 23 And changed the glory of the uncorruptible God into an image made like to corruptible man, and to birds, and fourfooted beasts, and creeping things. 24 Wherefore God also gave them up to uncleanness through the lusts of their own hearts, to dishonour their own bodies between themselves: 25 Who changed the truth of God into a lie, and worshipped and served the creature more than the Creator, who is blessed for ever. Amen. 26 For this cause God gave them up unto vile affections: for even their women did change the natural use into that which is against nature: 27 And likewise also the men, leaving the natural use of the woman, burned in their lust one toward another; men with men working that which is unseemly, and receiving in themselves that recompence of their error which was meet. 28 And even as they did not like to retain God in their knowledge, God gave them over to a reprobate mind, to do those things which are not convenient; 29 Being filled with all unrighteousness, fornication, wickedness, covetousness, maliciousness; full of envy, murder, debate, deceit, malignity; whisperers, 30 Backbiters, haters of God, despiteful, proud, boasters, inventors of evil things, disobedient to parents, 31 Without understanding, covenantbreakers, without natural affection, implacable, unmerciful: 32 Who knowing the judgment of God, that they which commit such things are worthy of death, not only do the same, but have pleasure in them that do them.

RELIGION

The United Nations has setup what is called the World Council of Churches which is a mixture of the four major world religions of Christianity, Islam, Buddhism and Hinduism.

World governments have dominion over the churches because of Tax Free Status laws which gives them sweeping powers. Also the child sexual abuse by the Catholic Church priests has given governments even more power under the guise of protecting children from predators by implementing safe church programs.

When the Antichrist does come to power he will use the state controlled church to be his platform, with tax free and having a political watchdog over the church because of abuse he will be able to declare himself god as it says 2 Thess 2:4 and have the law doing his bidding.

The level of deception in Christianity today is a huge problem. The problem has become worse since WW2 as the church has become very liberal. Liberal means that ministers and pastors no longer believe much of what the Bible teaches.

One of the main problems has been the theory of evolution which states that all life on earth was a biological accident over millions of years. We find now that in the name of science that it is fanciful to believe that God could create the world and all life in just six days.

Because of this exodus of belief we are at a time where faith has become rare and we have become a godless society. In 1859 Charles Darwin wrote his book called

Origin of Species. Many ungodly academics embraced and promoted this teaching because of their hatred of Christianity. Sadly over a period of time this teaching started to infiltrate seminaries and many started to question the six day creation, the virgin birth of Jesus and Noah's flood. Because naturally when leaders start to omit these fundamental and foundational truths then we will see the church start to lose members; which certainly has been the case.

One of the main problems with liberalism is that many different people have different ideas and views on what happened in the past.

One person will say that life on earth came by aliens whereas someone else will say God used evolution as a means of creation, and yet another will say that life came about by macro evolution which means that it happened very fast.

The point being that the academics can't even agree on how or when life on earth came into existence. They want us to believe their private theory and then that raises the question on who is really correct and how are we to know for sure because our salvation will depend of the fundamental question.

However in more modern times with the discovery of DNA and other amazing biological discoveries many scientists are abandoning the theory of evolution. There is a website called Dissent from Darwin (https://dissentfromdarwin.org/) where over 1200 scientist from different scientific background have added their name to the list.

What scientist are discovering is that miro-biology is so complex that it would be impossible for life to have come into being by accident as per the teaching of Darwinian Evolution.

You would think with this coming to light that liberalism would be on the decline in the church; however the opposite is the case.

None of these academics were there at creation, however the account in the Bible is a historical account of events that happened when God created the world 6000 years ago that have been handed down for us all to know.

These men who believe and teach this liberal doctrine have been prophesied about in the Bible. *2Ti 4:3 For a time will be when they will not endure sound doctrine, but they will heap up teachers to themselves according to their own lusts, tickling the ear.*

2Ti 4:4 And they will turn away their ears from the truth and will be turned to myths.

Because we are entering into the last days before the return of Jesus it is extremely important that we have and know the truth.

Many evangelical, Charismatic and Pentecostal church leaders are beginning to water down the scriptures. The biggest problem is what is called Israel replacement theology; this teaching states that Israel does not, and should not occupy the Holy Land. They believe that the church replaces Israel in all the Old Testament prophesies.

Ezekiel 38:8-9 state that in the last days when Israel has returned to its original land from the nations of the world they will be living in peace and we have seen Israel restored to the land which is a miracle as such a thing has never happened in history after such a long time.

Numbers 23:19 God is not human, that he should lie, not a human being, that he should change his mind. Does he speak and then not act? Does he promise and not fulfil?

The problem with this teaching is that will inevitably lead to anti-Semitic behaviour by Christians and a great example is the recent war against Hamas in Gaza.

The Palestinians fired thousands of rockets into Israel targeting the civilian population. Israel's military is far more advanced and better equipped than what the Palestinians are and so Israel retaliated with deadly force.

The problem is that the media are completely on the Palestinian side and thus they either lie, or promote the Palestinian propaganda. This then gets believed by ignorant population in the west and as would be expected many Christians get caught up in the fake news. Also because these Christians don't believe that Israel deserves the land they believe that the land should be divided up to make a sovereign Palestinian state.

This is against what the Bible teaches because God made covenant with Abraham that the land was Israel's and no-one else's.

Joel 3:2 I will gather all the nations and bring them down to the Valley of Jehoshaphat. And I will enter into judgment with them there, on behalf of my people and my heritage Israel, because they have scattered them among the nations and have divided up my land.
Christian's who support a two state solution which most replacement theology believers do are supporting a movement that is dedicated to the complete annihilation of every Jewish man woman and child. Even though they would not most likely support another holocaust because they are wanting two state solution it would align them with that outcome. The Palestinians have made it abundantly clear that they will never accept a two state solution as the only acceptable outcome for them is inhalation of all Jews. One only needs to look at the history of the proposed peace plans that the Palestinians have never kept; even when there was an agreement to divide the land.

SEXUALITY

Sexual laws are now written into nearly all governments including the World Economic Forum and the United Nations.

One hundred years ago sex was considered to be a word that was not used in mixed company, women were not allowed to wear a swim suit that exposed their lower legs and sex was extremely private.

By the 1920s the swim suits had been raised to just above the knees and inspectors were employed to measure them and if they were found to be too short the woman had to leave the beach.

The sexual revolution has really been a product of Hollywood and the entertainment industry, for example when Elvis Presley launched his first hit record 'That's Alright Mama' in July 1954 many churches protested of his dance routine on stage because he would gyrate his hips in a seductive way. It was that very same month and year the Johnson Amendment (501C3) was tabled and passed which prevented churches from speaking out about political issues.

Less than twenty years later in 1973 the rock band ACDC was launched which promoted satanic lyrics.

Now laws have been passed that completely empowers all form of sexual activity even on minors.

Abortion on demand was legalised from the 1960s onwards and is a form of contraception for the sexually promiscuous.

Homosexuality was legalised during this time with gay marriage starting around the 2000s.

Pornography and prostitution have both been legalised and now there are calls to lower the age for consensual sex.
To call our current social system Sodom and Gomorrah would be an understatement!

CLIMATE

World governments, United Nations and WEF all have departments, or bureaucracies of Climate Change. They are all saying exactly the same thing as if they reading from the same teleprompter and that is Climate Emergency or else the world will be extinct by 2030 and so they have termed this as the 2030 agenda. The problem is the agenda will have far greater negative impact on the world than any so called climate change. Every prediction that these people make never comes true. If they were paid for their accuracy they would have gone broke a long time ago.

During the 1960s it was we are going into another Ice-Age.

During the 1970s it was peak oil which predicted that oil would run out.

During the 1980s it was ozone layer was being destroyed.

During the 1990s and 2000s it was climate warming with Al Gore as the head crusader and warning the world would soon lose coastal areas because of melting ice.

Now it's just simple climate change and everyone will die unless we stop driving cars, using fertilizers.

Doesn't take a rocket scientist to see what will happen if they stop farming and transport for nearly eight billion people.

The greatest famine in human history with billions of people dying because of a fantasy.

Hmmm, maybe this is their plan!

It's amazing that the promoters of this lie is Education, Tech giants, Liberal Churches, Media, Entertainment and Business. These micro bureaucracies are united in their deception and maybe now there is enough evidence to call them the ten horns of the beast in John's Apocalypse.

To understand the level of deception one only needs to look at the so called climate emergency that is being preached by UN national governments and the lying media. After all they keep telling us that this is the reason for the great reset.

I worked in border protection in 2015 and was stationed at Manus Island PNG and the water levels there are the same as they have always been which is a contradiction to the rising sea levels they keep telling us about.

If anyone has been paying attention to the weather for the last couple of years they would realise that has cooled to what it was the decade before; yet we were forever been told that the weather will get much warmer.

We have experienced some very serve droughts over the past few years however that has more to do with Christian nations turning their backs on God. The Bible is very clear that if we do that then we can expect droughts and other calamities to happen. This is not because God wants to belt us with a big stick as punishment, He does this to try to get our attention to repent and turn back to Him.

Amo 4:7 And I have also withheld the rain from you, when there were yet three months to the harvest. And I

caused rain to fall on one city and caused it not to rain on another city; one piece was rained on, and the piece on which it did not rain dried up.
2 Chron 7:13-14. 1 Kings 17:1. Lev 26:19. Zech 14:17. All tell how God will cause it not to rain when we turn our backs on Him.
Even many church leaders and Christians have believed this climate emergency rubbish which only points out they are watching too much TV and swallowing the propaganda.
Summing up the level of deception that we are being constantly being fed, it covers every aspect our society and they are biology (Gender), government, Justice Departments, education, media, entertainment, religion, climate science and economics.
This puts us nearly the point of Jesus's return as the following scripture says.
Dan 8:25 ***he shall cause deceit to succeed in his hand and*** *he will consider himself superior.*
Daniel the prophet tells us that deceit will prosper when the Antichrist arrives and judging by the enormous amount of deception at every level of society this person must be here somewhere now. Jesus tells us something very similar in Matthew 24 that false Christs and prophets shall arise and deceive even the elect if that were possible.
This is also happening now with so many doomsayer climate alarmists preaching climate disaster by 2030. Not to mention all the people who prophesied Trumps re-election and some are still saying that Biden will lose

his seat to Trump because of all the corruption that we have witnessed.

MEDIA

Today's mainstream media are without doubt very dishonest and deceptive; they either only tell one side of the story or else they just simply lie about it.

18th January 2019 students from Covington Catholic High School were attending an anti-abortion rally in Washington DC and a student was wearing a maga hat and an elderly man approached the young man and was beating a drum and chanting in the boy's face because he didn't like Donald Trump. The young man stood there and smiled at the man as he was feeling threatened by the man beating the drum and chanting in his face.

This went viral on social media and when that happened the mainstream media started to run stories on the incident claiming that the young man was being disrespectful to the aggressive old man.

The reason was because nearly all the mainstream media utterly hate Donald Trump and will do and say anything to influence the population in the negative. This was a complete fabrication and lie. The young man's parents filed successful law suits against those media outlets.

On 29th January 2019 Jussie Smollett an actor living in Chicago laid a complaint to the CPD that some white supremacists had assaulted and racially vilified him. Without any evidence the media and democratic politicians went into overdrive calling white conservatives and Donald Trump racists. Shortly after that it was found that Smollett was lying about the incident. Even though he made extremely serious false allegations the Chicago Attorney General refused to lay charges against him and the media never back tracked or apologised for their lies.

Russia-gate was one of the first setups by the Washington establishment, media and the Democratic Party to overthrow an elected and sitting president. Clinton Foundation paid Christopher Steel an ex UK spy who hated Donald Trump to write up a fake dossier about Russia collusion connected to the Trump election campaign.

The media grabbed hold of this and made it their number one story for months without ever doing any investigative journalism.

Because of the huge coverage by the media the Democratic Party were able to force congress to employ a special counsel to investigate.

The special counsel headed by ex FBI director Robert Muller preceded with the greatest fraudulent witch hunt in US history. The people employed by the Muller were all partisan democrats and were extremely zealous for any conviction they could get.

George Papadopoulos and General Flynn were two innocent victims of the phony investigation. Generally the counsel investigators went after anyone who was connected to Donald Trump election.

After the failed bogus Muller investigation the democrats and Washington establishment tried to have Trump impeached. This attempt to overthrow Trump

was based on a phone call by Trump with the Ukraine Prime Minister.
Some crooked dealing by Hunter Biden, the son of now President of the United States Joe Biden's had happened and Trump wanted the Ukraine to investigate.
Hunter had been given a very high paid job for doing nothing and having no knowledge about the energy business.
His father was the vice president to Obama and this connection was very lucrative for the criminal energy company. When the Ukraine government employed a new Attorney General who was an honest man he wanted to do an investigation into the cooked company and dealings with the Biden's; Joe Biden the then vice president bragged on TV news that he had the prime minister of Ukraine sack the new attorney general.
The news reporter never even questioned or challenged the statement and by doing so was also guilty in the crime and deception.
During the 2020 election campaign Hunter Biden the son of candidate Joe Biden had a laptop computer exposed to the media about his dealings with China and the Ukraine with his father's involvement.
The emails from the laptop revealed that Hunter had been involved with in some wild sexual misconduct and drug abuse and as soon as these become known to the public the media went to work to cover-up the crimes of the president and his son.

They called it Russian misinformation and social media banned any mention of the laptop at all. The comparison to watching the news on TV, or buying a newspaper is the same as going down town and inviting the worst pathological liar back to your home and has him sit in the corner of your lounge where your TV stands and tell you a pack of lies while you are eating your evening meal.

ENTERTAINMENT

The entertainment industry is renowned for its pro-Marxist view and hatred of Christianity. They are always promoting satanic movies and music and will always make anything godly look evil. They have fulfilled what Isaiah the prophet said in Isa 5: 20.

They call good evil and evil good. The hatred by actors and singers has been on display for the world to see and this hatred drives these people to do and say anything that would lead the public away from conservative Christian values. They use all the great acting abilities to deceive the population.

Robert De Niro the great and legendary Hollywood star went on YouTube on 11th November 2016 spewing out terrible profanities and threatening to punch President Donald Trump in the face.

Kathy Griffin Hollywood comedian and celebrity made up a bloodied image of a severed head in the look alike of Trump.

On the 28th January 2017 Madonna in a public address at a demonstration against Trump stated that she often thinks about blowing up the Whitehouse.

Back in the nineteen fifties Hollywood was a completely different world to what it is today. Wonderful movies mere produced that were about the Bible and our Christian heritage. Movies like Samson and Delilah staring Victor Mature, and the Ten Commandments staring Charlton Heston and Edward G Robertson. These were block buster movies with huge budgets and viewing.

The sexual content of modern movies leaves nothing hidden and has become normal for a population that has become so corrupt and their corruption seems to have desensitised any logical thinking.

HEALTH

The World Health Organization (WHO) lied and covered up for the Chinese communist party about the source of the Wuhan Covid-19 pandemic. The Wuhan scientists who blew the whistle about the fact that the virus escaped, or was released from the laboratory were very courageous to inform the world of the true source however they went missing and have not been seen or heard of since.

When some news outlets broke the real story of the pandemic social media and the lying mainstream went into overdrive to silence and also cover-up for the Chinese Communist Party calling anyone who said that virus came from the laboratory a racist or conspiracy nut.

The responses to the pandemic by governments around the world have been outrageous and evil. The lockdowns have no scientific validity at all as never in the history of the human race have governments locked healthy people up. The normal and most practical response is to quarantine the sick while allowing life to continue as normal.

Many Doctors and research scientist have been saying the same thing from the beginning. The Great Barrington Declaration which is a petition signed by over forty eight thousand scientists and medical practitioners around the world has been completely ignored by these evil politicians.

https://gbdeclaration.org/signatures/. The Great Barrington Declaration is a statement advocating an

alternative approach to the COVID-19 pandemic which involves "Focused Protection" of those most at risk and seeks to avoid or minimize the societal harm of the COVID-19 lockdowns. Hydroxychloroquine a drug that is primarily for the treatment of malaria has been widely available as an effective treatment 1955 when it was passed in the USA.
Very soon after the outbreak of the pandemic it was found the Hydroxychloroquine a very effective drug to fight the virus.
When this was information was first released to the public governments around the world banned Doctors from prescribing this to their patients who were suffering from Covid-19.
The people that would most benefit from this would be the big pharmaceutical companies who are making the Covid-19 vaccines and the dirty politicians media companies who are been paid for their support.
In Victoria when a few cases have been reported the state government have declared a state of emergency and locked the state down and only allowing people to leave their home for essential reasons.
They also made mask wearing mandatory for anyone leaving their home. Masks have been proven to be useless against the virus because the holes in the mask are a lot bigger than what the Covid virus is. The comparison is that it would be like using wire mesh used to make a chicken coop as a mosquito net. The mosquitos would not even touch the sides the same as the virus to the face mask.

Since the vaccine has been distributed there is growing pressure from media, health bureaucrats, corporations, universities and politicians to make the jab a legal requirement to travel, go to school, work or even shop. However the most obvious question is; if you have been vaccinated against the virus why would there be a concern from someone who has not been vaccinated? After all isn't that the purpose of the vaccine to protect them from the virus?
From the very early days when the pandemic broke out many research scientists have been saying that the virus is really only a danger to the very sick or the elderly and that we must protect these people.
The very young are hardly effected by the virus at all and yet with all the information that we now know we are still living under a state of emergency with all sorts of draconian rules that are a total overreach of power by evil politicians and government bureaucrats.
Hospitals now offer pregnant women abortions which were illegal but now they are government funded and even promoted as a way of combatting climate change by keeping the population down.
Hospitals were a place to receive care for sick but now they have become human abattoirs by murdering innocent children.
They are 'Infant Abattoirs' because they kill babies for profit as their body parts are sold to companies for research and other purposes.

Add to that the butchering and mutilation of children for sexual realignment and hospitals are a satanic tool that is far from what they started out to be.

BUSINESS FINANCE

One of the greatest impacts of the Covid-19 virus has been on the economy because of the lockdowns. Governments have openly shown their hypocrisy and deception by allowing large corporations to remain open while shutting down small business. There have been no restrictions on numbers going into the large supermarket chain while small businesses were shut down and going broke.

During the shutdown governments have been handing out huge amounts of money to people while they remained locked up in their homes creating the greatest debt in history. Because people have had extra cash there has been an online spending spree which has created a shortage of some goods because factories were closed.

Small business is the greatest financial contributor to any democratic society and these closures will cause a massive crash and depression sometime in the future. Government economists would be well aware of the effects of the closure of small business and yet for no logical reason they have taken this action. This really makes you wonder if this was their plan from the beginning.

And if so, why?

Nearly all financial gurus are predicting a massive financial crash because the complete mismanagement by government. This is on display for all to see practically in the USA under the Biden administration where they have all but totally wrecked the economy

there. John Kerry the special envoy to the United Nation for climate change has declared that the US will move towards climate change measures.
The plan involves dramatically increasing the power of government through expansive new social programs like the Green New Deal and using vast regulatory schemes and government programs to coerce corporations into supporting left-wing causes.
World Economic Forum WEF under Klaus Schwab is the mastermind of the Great Reset which is what is heading up this move.
It is all under what they term a climate emergence which they say will cause a global disaster by the year 2030 unless drastic and definitive action to reduce carbon is not taken.
They talk about a reset and the only way something is reset is when it is broken. If they want to reset the economy then it must be in a state of brokenness first. This then must imply that the now existing financial system must have to be broken in order to reset it to something new.
Before this is done then the public must be on board for the changes otherwise there would be a revolution and they would never get the reset they want. With this in mind they would have to use all means available to them to gain the trust of the world's populations.
This would be done by starting a brainwashing program by the media, education, government and entertainment. Then give the population large amounts of cash and tell them you are locking them up for their

own safety. Seems a pretty good deal for the government to tell us to stay home and we will pay your wage; like a dream come true!

Maybe it's not a dream at all but rather a nightmare in reality. You have heard that saying. 'When it seems too good to be true it is.'

There is nothing for free in this world except salvation through the Lord Jesus Christ.

If it's not a blessing that we are receiving from the government then it must be a curse and we can be assured that we are soon to embark on the worst times ever recorded in history.

THE ANTICHRIST

There has been a lot of interest in whom the Antichrist is and when he will appear, even the secular are interested in this subject as they continue to make movies that reference this subject.

The Bible gives us some clues about his character and what he will do. We know that he will overtake, or replace three of the micro kings of the ten horns on the beast Daniel 7:20 and if the ten bureaucracies are the ten horns of this End-Time beast then we should expect that three of these will be used or replaced by the Antichrist.

The three that would serve the Antichrist to come to his ultimate power are Law, Technology and Religion.

The Antichrist will need to have the law so that he can change it for the purpose of his power and he will need technology because that is how he will control the population though microchips and computer database.

The two horns that are on his head described in Revelation 13:11 are representative of some type of dominion or power and the obvious powers would be political and religion and religion would be the third horn that he takes control of. 2Thes 2:4 tells us that he does sit on God's throne and declares himself to be God. He would need to have complete political power of the whole world.

Some of the characteristics of the Antichrist are, pride, homosexual, cruel, very deceitful and have some supernatural satanic powers. He also makes a covenant

with Israel for peace and he is very charismatic and likable.
Judging by what is happening in the world at the moment there would be little doubt that the man of sin is already walking amongst us however he will not be able to be identified until halfway through the tribulation.
An obvious venue for his arrival would be the United Nations or the World Economic Forum as these are powerful global institutions and would best serve his needs.
His rise to attain this type of complete global dominance would have to come from a crisis of the likes that has never been seen before, like a nuclear holocaust and severe famine which appears the world is on the verge of at this very moment.
The USA is provoking Russia into a nuclear conflict and China is making moves for global expansion which would mean military conflict. Added to that North Korea is itching to use their nuclear weapons on America and Iran nearly has developed their first nuclear weapon which they have sworn to use on Israel.
The insane green policies of stopping farmers using fertilizers and banning fossil fuels will take the world into the greatest famine ever recorded.
There is no question that the world is on the verge of the greatest human crisis that has ever happened and Jesus described it as follows.

Mat 24:15 *Therefore when you see the abomination of desolation, spoken of by Daniel the prophet, stand in the*

*holy place (whoever reads, let him understand). 16 Then
let those in Judea flee into the mountains. 17 Let him on
the housetop not come down to take anything out of his
house; 18 nor let him in the field turn back to take his
clothes. 19 And woe to those who are with child, and to
those who give suck in those days! 20 But pray that
your flight is not in the winter, nor on the sabbath
day; 21 for then shall be great tribulation, such as has
not been since the beginning of the world to this time;
no, nor ever shall be. 22 And unless those days should
be shortened, no flesh would be saved. But for the
elect's sake, those days shall be shortened.*

7 CHURCHES

There has been much written about the seven Churches written in chapters two and three in Revelation.

I have read it thousands of times myself and could not really make sense of what the message is.

Then I decided to read it purely from an End-Time perspective and just let the book say what it says. In other words not try and make it fit an idea, historical event or newspaper headline.

Ephesus, Smyrna, and Pergamum the first three churches John wrote to seemed to be historical events and address the emergence of false prophets and liberalism in the church.

The church of Ephesus left their first love however Jesus was pleased that they tested people who called themselves apostles and they hated the work of the Nicolaitans which Jesus was very pleased with. Jesus says He hates this practice which is very strong language to use.

There is some dispute about what they were exactly guilty of other than they diluted the word of God with some pagan practices, this is the same as liberal theologians do today on how they adopt the theory of evolution and other pagan worldly practices.

The Smyrna church was without fault and was to go through some time of persecution as Jesus mentioned it would last ten days Rev 2:10.

Pergamum was a historical church also because Jesus never mentioned that He would be returning. They did begin to allow false prophets and pagan liberal people

into their church and Jesus threatened them that He would come and fight against them by the Word of His mouth.
But from Thyatira to Laodicea the last four churches Jesus was defiantly describing the church in the last days.
Jesus says to Thyatira Rev 2:25. (Hold onto what you have until I come.)
To Sardis Jesus said to wake up or you won't know at what hour I come Rev: 3:3.
To Philadelphia He tells them to hold on to what they have till He comes so that no one can take their crown.
However the situation is very grim for the Church of Laodicea as they finish up being a pile of vomit. Only those individuals who answer the door will be saved.
Only three Churches will be represented in the End-Time because Laodicea being the forth is vomited out.
This really does give clarity to what's happening to the church in these times.
1. Thyatira will be the church that goes through the Great Tribulation and we know this because Jesus said it. ***Rev 2:22*** *Behold, I will cast her into a bed, and them that commit adultery with her into **great tribulation**, except they repent of their deeds.*
2. Sardis is the church that is asleep and Matthew twenty five talks about the ten virgins and that five of them are prevented from entering into the wedding feast because they had no oil in their lamps. Some in this church are dressed in white Rev 3:4 indicating they are waiting and ready to receive the bridegroom.

3. Philadelphia will be the raptured church as it is awake and ready to receive the Lord.
This is played out in the parable of the parable of the wedding banquet in Matt 22:1-14 as we see that the Lord announces that the wedding feast is ready and he sends out invites to all the guests but they refuse for various reasons.
The reality of the reasons is the same as the case of the story of Lot's wife when she looked back. The lights of the world are shinning too bright and they don't want to leave their worldly situation.
This situation takes a bit of getting the head around because here we have the greatest event in all history about to happen and much of the church is far more invested in the lights of the world rather than the true Light of heaven; Jesus Christ.
No wonder he said to them "Depart from me I never knew you."

RAPTURE

We are fast approaching the greatest church event in all history and that is the rapture of the church. There is much debate about when or even if this will take place. I have read much and watched countless hours of teaching on the subject and I could never come to a sure conclusion what was the correct sequence of events.

For a long time I favoured a Mid-Tribulation rapture because I couldn't see how God could let the church of the hook when it has been so derelict in its duty and responsibility here on earth.

Jesus strongly emphasises in Matthew, Mark and Luke to keep lookout Matt 24:45-47, Mark 13:32-36 and Luke 21:36. In Matt 24:45 Jesus tells us that we must be teaching about His return. In 2Thess 5:4 Paul tells us that we won't know the day or hour but we will know the season.

Sadly we see that most of the evangelical church refuses to even talk about End-Times and political event that affect all our lives.

There will be an early departure from the earth by those believers that are paying attention to the signs of the time and talking about them.

There is some evidence for an early departure or pre-trib and mid-trib rapture and we will examine them now.

The two churches that will go thought the Great Tribulation are both Thyatira and Sardis; Thyatira because this church she made legal covenant with government to help them with the cost of running a church, this really is the king of Sodom partnership. Jesus said that because you do that I will put you on a bed of suffering and that Thyatira will go the great Tribulation. Rev 2:22.

With Sardis it is a different story because that church was sound asleep. Jesus equates that to being dead Rev 3:1. Some organisational and individual churches may be suffering with both the Thyatira and Sardis syndrome.

That symptom would be that this church does not engage in End-Time teaching and is signed up with all sorts of government programs to help fund their churches.

As mentioned before Laodicea is a nothing church other than a few stragglers that will be answer the door to Jesus. Churches that best fit this profile would be liberal woke churches that have labelled most of the Bible as fiction.

No wonder Jesus told the five virgins who never had any oil that He did not know them. They failed to take the essential ingredient with them so that they could find their way to where the feast was to be held.

They just didn't because they failed to be excited about the Lords coming. Any woman who is about to be married is super excited as it is the most important day of her life. The church that is not teaching and super excited about the appearance of the bride-groom is not worthy to be a bride. Also Revelation chapter eleven gives us further look into an early departure for the bride. We see the angel hands John a measuring tool to measure inside the temple, the altar and those that worship there, but the outer court is left for the gentiles to trample on for forty two months.

The fact that those who are outside the temple for a given time period to measure, or count the believers infers that the people counted inside the temple are separated.

This also corresponds with the parable of the ten virgins as the ones that have oil and are awake looking for the bridegroom are those that went into the wedding feast, or in this case are counted inside the temple, and the five that had no oil are locked out of the wedding feast.

The good news is for those locked out is that they now have a great commission to fulfil and that is the completion of preaching the gospel to every tribe and tongue and nation Matt 24:14.

Rev11:7 says that when the two witnesses have finished their testimony and they will be killed by the Antichrist means that they must finish the task of preaching the gospel to the nations before they are silenced.

This will be the saints murdered through the Great Tribulation and finally get their white robes that they missed out because they refused to pay attention to Bible prophesy.

Rev 6:9 When He opened the fifth seal, I saw under the altar the souls of those who had been slain for the word of God and for the testimony which they held. Rev 6:10 And they cried with a loud voice, saying, "How long, O

Lord, holy and true, until You judge and avenge our blood on those who dwell on the earth?"
Rev 6:11 Then a ***white robe was given to each of them****; and it was said to them that they should rest a little while longer, until both the number of their fellow servants and their brethren, who would be killed as they were, was completed.*
The churches dependence on the government for their financial existence is no different to the unfaithful bride. She is in covenant with the king of Sodom.
Not long after I retired I was investing in the stock-market as a means of income because I was running a mission to the Solomon Islands. At the beginning I was doing really well and following a set pattern for investment.
Then all of sudden I had a couple of losses that was over a thousand dollars and I cried out to God that I was doing it help with the mission.
When I was in prayer explaining my case the Lord revealed to me how much it broke His heart that I didn't rely on him for income for the mission. I felt His broken heart and it really shocked me that He was so affected. However the Philadelphian church is a very weak End-Time church that holds the keys of David and will escape the Great-Tribulation. Best way to describe this church are as churches that are not aligned with government and are constantly examining the scriptures and current political events that may be relevant to the return of Jesus. If Thyatira, Sardis and Philadelphia are all End-Time churches, which they because Jesus mentions His

return for these churches and two are going to go through the Great Tribulation and one isn't then it's only natural to assume that there will be either a pre, mid-trib rapture because one has been taken.
The angel that hands John the scroll in Revelation ten is very good indicator for early rapture because he says to John in verse six and seven that at the beginning and in the days when the seventh angel sounds his trumpet the mystery of God will be complete. Three very important points here are.

1. He says the mystery of God will be complete. The resurrection of the dead was not a mystery in the Old Testament because the Pharisees believed that there was to be a resurrection of the dead on the last day. The angel was obviously talking about a different mystery. This is the same mystery that Paul mentions in 1Cor 15:51 and that is we won't all sleep, but will be changed in the twinkling of an eye.
2. The angel says at the beginning of the trumpet blast this mystery will be complete. This seems to say that while this angel is sounding his trumpet there will be other events on earth happening after rapture.
3. Also the angel says that in the days when he sounds his trumpet which is plural meaning that he will be sounding his trumpet longer than one day. Doesn't say how long that will be, however if angel was to sound a trumpet it wouldn't be impossible for him to sound it for days, months of years. They are spiritual and don't need to draw breath as we do.

The Great Tribulation will be the greatest and most horrific time in the history of the human race and it would be difficult to imagine that the trumpet would sound throughout this time nonstop.
Similar to an air raid siren sounding to warn people of an incoming air attack, whoever this is a warning from the realm of the spirit to warn people what has been released onto the earth. Jesus adds some light to this when he said in Matt 24:15 when He said that when you see the abomination that causes desolation; the emphasis is when you see.
He didn't say when the Abomination that causes desolation is setup, or established. Most people will fall in behind the Antichrist and march in lockstep throughout the three and half year period.
This will be a revelation for those who have had their eyes opened to the truth and in order for a spiritual awakening of this magnitude the trumpet would have to be sounded non-stop throughout this difficult time.
The trumpet was used by Israel in the wilderness to blow different tunes for different events Num 10:1-10.
They used trumpet blasts to move out of campsite or to have a meeting, the trumps has been replaced by radio communications. When armies went into battle they would sound different tunes for different actions that needed to be deployed.
The defeat of the great harlot in Revelation eighteen and nineteen point to an early rapture because in Rev 19: 6 we see the bride is made ready in white garment for the wedding feast. The harlot is killed by the

Antichrist because it is the ten kings that as the scripture says they will eat her flesh and burn her body Rev 17:16.
The Antichrist is killed when Jesus returns on the white horse Rev 19:19 which is the battle of Armageddon which is a later battle indicating that the defeat of the harlot and rapture happen before Armageddon.
This is exciting news for those believers that are awake and watching for the Lords return, however there may be a bit too much weight put on the rapture event itself rather that the focus being on the Lords appearance.
It really is understandable because what the rapture means is that we don't have to go through the Great Tribulation and that's absolutely worth being very excited about.

TWO WITNESESS

Many people believe that the two witnesses will be Moses and Elijah as Jesus mentioned that Elijah would come and restore all things in the last days Mark 9:5 and Mal 4:2.

In Luke 1:7 the angel tells Zachariah John the Baptists father that John would come in the spirit of Elijah and so by this word we would have to assume that the two witnesses will come in the spirit of Elijah.

Rev 11:3 I will send my two witnesses dressed in sackcloth, and they will proclaim God's message during those 1, 260 days."

*Rev 11:4 The two witnesses are the two olive trees and the **two lamps that stand** before the Lord of the earth.*

Rev 11:5 If anyone tries to harm them, fire comes out of their mouths and destroys their enemies; and in this way whoever tries to harm them will be killed.

The scripture tells us exactly who the two witnesses will be as they are referred to as the two candlesticks and in in Rev 1:20 which is two churches.

*Rev 1:20 Here is the secret meaning of the seven stars that you see in my right hand, and of the seven gold lampstands: the seven stars are the angels of the seven churches, and the seven **lampstands are the seven churches**.*

The two olive trees would represent the Holy Spirit that they are anointed with to do this very difficult ministry. Also for the two witnesses to be only two men would be completely impractical to preach to the whole world. It must be the church that takes the Gospel into the world

because part of the prophesying will be preaching the gospel to a world in the grip of the worst time ever.
To further point out that these two witnesses are the Thyatira and Sardis churches is that they are dressed in sackcloth and the only reason why they are in sackcloth is because they mourning.
The Rapture would be the most devastating event for these believers that were left behind; they would be absolutely gutted when they saw many of their brothers and sisters in the Lord taken to heaven for the wedding supper.
Many will be so upset that they will simply give up and these will be part of the great falling away 2Thess 2:3; however those that see the mistake they made will be fearless warriors for the Lord and the He will use them mightily.
Many people believe that 2 Thess 2:7, that which is taken out of the way is the Holy Spirit. (Indicating the removal of the Holy Spirit will allow the Antichrist to arise to his full power) However that doesn't make sense because for the two witnesses to have their ministry and to be void of the Holy Spirit would mean that it would be a powerless ministry and when you read Revelation eleven it is anything but powerless.
The taking out of the way referral by Paul here is talking about the final defeat of the two witnesses (Churches) Rev 13:7, & Rev 11:10
That is why the nations of the world celebrated sending gifts to each other because finally they don't have to put up with these Christians. We can see that this is

already beginning to happen with hostility from government, entertainment and media ramping up towards believers.
The city that their bodies lie in is figuratively called Sodom and Egypt is most likely the great harlot Babylon written in Rev 17 because it was where the Lord was crucified as well and it does say in Rev 17:6 that the great harlot was drunk on the blood of the saints. We know that Jesus wasn't crucified in either Sodom or Egypt.

MYSTERY BABYLON THE GREAT HARLOT
When reading through Revelation there seems at first look that there are some contradictions of just who Babylon the Harlot is. The great harlot is killed by the ten kings who belong to the End-Time One World Government. Rev 17:16.
However when reading through Rev 16 where the 7 bowls of God's wrath is poured out we see that it is the return of Jesus brings an end to the Babylonian rule Rev 16:17-19. And again in chapter nineteen we see the Jesus returning with the armies of heaven for the last great battle of Armageddon and the breast and the false prophet are thrown into the Lake of Fire.
Revelation is really giving two individuals the identity of Babylon. The first one is the Great Harlot that rides on the back of the beast. And the second one is the beast, or otherwise known as the One World Government, or beast that comes out of the sea Rev 13:1.
Because the Babylon the harlot is killed first we need to get an understanding just who this might represent in these last days.
The main beast, or beasts described in both the book of Daniel and Revelation are world kingdoms, or powers. What is being described here is a political organisation. Harlot Babylon is on the back of this beast and she is responsible for the murder of people who follow God Rev 17:6.
Because she riding on the back it must be concluded that she is directing the main political kingdom or world power and seems that her main task is to murder God's

people. The comparison is the same as someone riding a horse.
The horse is very large but the rider on the back is in complete control.
Jezebel is the Babylonian spirit at work and she is our understanding in identifying this End-Time power.
King Ahab was a weak king and his wife Jezebel controlled him in his Kingship.
She had Naboth killed so Ahab could have his property; when Naboth refused to sell the property to King Ahab he got depressed so Jezebel murdered Naboth. Jezebel also persecuted the church by murdering the prophets 1 Kings 18:4.
She changed Israel's religion to Baal worship and child sacrifice.
She is the perfect picture of the harlot riding on the beast.
Ahab represents the beast, or political power and Jezebel is the rider steering every political move towards evil.
Today's church has mistakenly identified the Jezebel spirit as a spirit within the church that is overly controlling. This is a mistake because clearly the Jezebel spirit is a spirit that controls government to persecute believers. It is an outside evil force rather than inside one.
One of the most important aspects of warfare is the gathering of intelligence. To understand the enemy and what his movements are will in most circumstances win the battle. This jezebel spirit is a major problem for the

modern church and unless the church awakens then we will continue down the road of defeat.
To explain it clearer this evil spirit is the dominating force that the church is persecuted by western governments around the world.
She is on the back of our political leaders!
We have been busy over the past fifty years delivering this spirit from inside our church walls and all the time she is laughing at us because we don't understand what is really happening.
To put this practical terms for today and what's happening to the free world in both politics and church. The great prostitute (Jezebel spirit) is mounting the free governments of the world to force them to come after the Church of Jesus Christ with a vengeance; just as Jezebel did in the days of King Ahab.
As world democracy transform into global Marxism so does the evil power that rides this beast.
The question has to be asked about what relationship the modern church has with evil beast and the woman who rides it?
It's very likely that this evil spirit mystery Babylon was birthed under the rule of King Ahab 875-854 BC because he married that pagan woman whose father was a prophet of Baal.
King Ahab unwittingly released an evil spirit into the world that would reap havoc throughout the rest of history. This evil untidy has been riding on the backs of political powers like kings and governments that were ruled and controlled by the Catholic.

The Catholic Church was responsible for the murder of millions of saints throughout the Dark and Middle Ages. The Inquisition torture chambers were testimony to their brutality and cruelty. And in these modern times we see this evil spirit ride on the backs of our democratic governments.

A great example of this evil spirit at work now is Daniel Andrews the Victorian Premier determination to come after the believers for what they believe. He recently had legislation passed that makes it a crime to pray for a homosexual with a maximum penalty of ten years imprisonment.

This doesn't take into account the hate speech laws that effectively ban the Word of God from society.

SATAN'S EVICTION Chapter twelve in Revelation gives us description and insight to what is going with the eviction of Satan from heaven. To understand this chapter it must follow the trend that's already beginning to emerge and that is the rapture of the church and great tribulation.

Firstly after Jesus is caught up to heaven Rev 12:5 there is a time gap of two thousand years before going onto the next verse.

We know this because the church or Israel has not been in wilderness environment for that period of time because wilderness really means a time of doing things tough.

This rather is the beginning of the seven year tribulation because God cares for the woman for a three and half year period.

This really means that the rapture probably won't happen until that time is up because in order for the bride to be allowed in heaven Satan must be cast out of heaven and cease to be prosecuting attorney, or accuser of the brethren.

That doesn't happen until the midway mark of the tribulation and this will be most likely when Satan has overplayed his hand by messing with the human gene and transforming nations into Sodom and Gomorrah at government levels where Satan rules from. It is then that God has the legal right to end Satan's tenure as Prosecuting Attorney and then war is waged against him in heaven and he is finally cast down to the earth. As was mentioned before we are all on trial here on earth

until Satan is removed and access to heaven won't legally happen until that event fulfilled.
Not forgetting that we are held in a holding cell (Our fleshly body) and are on trial for our lives because if we are found guilty then we will face a death penalty which is eternity in hell and separation from God and our final judgement doesn't happen until after death of our physical bodies.
At the midway point the churches that are left will be the two witnesses, or the Churches of Thyatira and Sardis and their experience will be a wilderness one to put it mildly.
Satan goes after the woman and spews water from his mouth to overtake her. That water will be deception and extremely powerful deception as Jesus mentioned all the way through Matthew twenty four.
The good news is that heaven and those in heaven will be rejoicing because it says that the now salvation has come to God. This really means the taking up of the Church for wedding feast.
We see that Jesus receives power because the accuser of the brethren has been cast out. This really demonstrates level of power and authority that Satan had over the world and its people because of the fall of man.
God could have ended Satan in a heartbeat but he was bound by His own law.
The word that is used for the power that Jesus received was the Greek word exousia. Which means force, *capacity*, *competency*, *freedom*, or (objectively) *mastery*

(concretely *magistrate, superhuman, potentate, token of control*), delegated *influence:* - authority, jurisdiction, power, strength. It is at this point that Jesus comes into His full authority of King of Kings and Lord of Lords. Chapter thirteen we see that Satan is standing on the sea shore and it is here that the full powers of evil are released upon the earth with the emergence of the Antichrist and false prophet. The beast with the wounded head that comes back to life may be the resurrection of communism as we are witnessing now with the emergence of the Marxist One World Government we are seeing being established in real time under the United Nations and the World Economic Forum.

Communism suffered is death blow with the fall of the Soviet Union from 1989-1992; and it seems that it came back to life when they released the Covid-19 weapon in March of 2020.

This being the case then we can expect to see a rapid move by all nations towards dictatorship control over the populations and then they will introduce a mark that people will be required to have to buy and sell.

The fourteenth chapter again continues the unfolding of information to what will happen during the Great Tribulation.

Verse six tell of an angel flying through mid-air having the everlasting Gospel to preach; this is great encouragement for the two churches whose job it to do this task as they will have special angel assigned so that

this will be completed before that allocated time has passed.
The second angel confirms the fall of western governments which is the mystery Babylon and the third angel warns that anyone who is to receive the mark of the beasty 666 will spend eternity in the Lake of Fire.
Then in verse thirteen we are told of a very special event and that is the resurrection of the dead in Christ and the rapture.
Rev 14:13 Then I heard a voice from heaven saying to me, "Write: ***'Blessed are the dead who die in the Lord from now on****.' " "Yes," says the Spirit, "that they may rest from their labours, and their works follow them."*
It is at this point that the seventh trumpet is sounded because there is only one blessing a dead person can have and that is to be raised from the dead.
Because life on earth will continue that tells us that the seventh trumpet gets sounded well before the second coming of Jesus and this will most likely be around the middle of the Great Tribulation.

ARMAGEDDON
There has been much written about the battle of Armageddon which has developed many different theories about where and when it will take place. There are some that dismiss it as only a myth and won't happen.
God's wrath and Armageddon can't happen until the Gospel is finally preached to every tribe tongue and nation because judgement can't happen until everyone knows that they are guilty of sin.
This only happens when people have heard the Gospel, then it is up to the individual to accept the truth or reject it.
I thought it would be good to try to develop a case based on the Word of God says and see what we can make from that.
The word Armageddon comes from a place in Israel called Megiddo and that is a strategic battle field situated in the northern part of Israel where empires won and lost battle as it was a gateway from east to west in the ancient world; whoever held this ground was the dominating army.
The word Armageddon is only used in Rev 16:16 however the battle is described in many places in the Old Testament; for example Ezekiel talks about it in depth in Eze 38 & 39, also Zechariah mentions it in 13 & 14. Daniel speaks about it but not as directly as Ezekiel.
Like understanding any conflict we need to know who the participants will be and Ezekiel tells us that Persis,

Gog and Magog, Put, Gomer, Meshech, Tubal and Beth-Togarmah Eze 38:1-6.
John indicates that China and North Korea may be involved in this alliance as well as he says that waters of the Euphrates will be dried up to make way for the kings of the east Rev 16:12. The Euphrates would need to be crossed for armies coming from Asia.
The general agreement is that these armies that Ezekiel is talking about are from Russia, Turkey, Iran and surrounding nation. Over the centuries nations change their names and borders because of war and conquest.
The really interesting part of these prophesies are who is not mentioned in this conflict. Muslim countries, Eastern Europe and Asia are all mentioned but western nations like America, Western Europe and pacific Asia (Australia & New Zealand) aren't mentioned at all.
The reason is because there has been a total collapse and annihilation of these nations as these nations are Mystery Babylon the Great Mother of Prostitutes and Abomination of the Earth Rev 17:5.
America was the leader of this coalition of nations and unfortunately she led the way in abominable practices like same sex marriage, homosexualization of children on mass, abortion and many other immoral practices that they enshrined into law.
They allowed the great harlot to ride them to destruction just the same as when Jezebel did to King Ahab in ancient Israel.
America and the free world was founded on the Bible and Ten Commandments and was a great light of hope

for the whole world. These nations sent missionaries into the pagan world to proclaim the good news of the Gospel of Jesus Christ.
It is so sad to see the state of our once great nations have descended into as our governments have become so corrupt and evil that God will not allow these practices to continue and will bring swift judgement upon us for these most grievous sins.
The end of the great harlot came about by the ten kings of the beast Rev 17:16 when they eat her flesh and burn her body.
We can see these alliances being setup now with Russia, Turkey, Iran, North Korea and China setting up a coalition. We see that they are even looking at dumping the USA dollar for a gold standard. Just to add fuel to the fire the Biden administration provoking both China and Russia into a global conflict.
God gave me a dream on January 28th 2021 of Chinese jets bombing Melbourne; the dream was in bright colours and the explosion so loud that I was awakened and I was very startled.
Further evidence of western democracies being the great harlot Mystery Babylon is their great wealth that they have acquired since WW2.
Rev 18:11 "And the merchants of the earth will weep and mourn over her, for no one buys their merchandise anymore:
Rev 18:12 merchandise of gold and silver, precious stones and pearls, fine linen and purple, silk and scarlet, every kind of citron wood, every kind of object of ivory,

every kind of object of most precious wood, bronze, iron, and marble;
Rev 18:13 and cinnamon and incense, fragrant oil and frankincense, wine and oil, fine flour and wheat, cattle and sheep, horses and chariots, and bodies and souls of men.
The battle of Armageddon is the very last war that will usher in the return of the Lord and so there is an order of events to happen. As pointed out before the harlot is killed by the beast before this war is fought against Israel.
There is no indication when the coalition of nation will destroy the western nations but judging by current events it can't be too far away.
The remnant of the western nations will most likely be the Churches of Thyatira and Sardis and they are the two witnesses dressed in sackcloth, however the Antichrist will make war them and kill them, Rev 13:7, Rev 11:10.
It is at this point that the seven bowls of God's wrath is poured out upon those nations leading up to that final battle and as you read through these events we see that people just cursed God rather than repenting, Rev 16:1-21.
The size of this army is amazing as it says in Eze 38:9 that Gog and Magog will be like a cloud covering the ground. The Russian coalition of nations can muster an army of over five million active personal.
With tensions between east and west and the formidable size of their armies and the moral state of

western nations it's not that difficult to see what will soon take place. Jesus said that if we pay attention and have a good heart attitude then we will be able to read the signs of the time.

Matt16:3 And early in the morning you say, 'It is going to rain, because the sky is red and dark.' You can predict the weather by looking at the sky, but you cannot interpret the signs concerning these times!

Mat 16:4 How evil and godless are the people of this day! You ask me for a miracle? No! The only miracle you will be given is the miracle of Jonah." So he left them and went away.

Muslim nations will be part of the armies that make up Gog and Magog however Islam will not be the dominant religion that this evil army will ride on.

In Daniel 11 we see that Antichrist will not follow any god but rather declare himself to be God 2 Thess 2:4 and there seems to be some indication that will be homosexual as in Daniel eleven he says that he has no regard for the god of women.

The world council of churches that are attempting to bring together all religion under one umbrella for the United Nations and the World Economic Forum for the One World Government will come to nothing because all these false religions will have to bow down to the man of sin, or the Antichrist.

This huge army will invade Israel and it seems that their goal is to plunder Israel because some other nations say that when it is revealed what they are doing when

Tarshish asks Gog and Magog that very question Eze 38:13.
However the main reason would be the hatred towards by nearly all nations of the world. In the United Nation General Assembly Israel is the most voted against nation in the world; even New Zealand has been a very strong advocate for a two state solution which is in opposition to the Word of God.
*Joe 3:2 I will gather all the nations and bring them to the Valley of Judgment. There I will judge them for all they have done to my people. They have scattered the Israelites in foreign countries and **divided Israel, my land.***
Many Muslim nations have promised to completely kill every last Jewish person and Israel has been the most persecuted people in the world throughout history. This should be no surprise as this hatred is driven by Satan he himself as knows if he can destroy Israel then he can prevent the return of Jesus in the second coming because the prophesies cannot be fulfilled.
The prophesies are law and must be fulfilled otherwise God can't allow Jesus to return because it would be against His own Law. The good news is that Israel will not be destroyed under Satan's watch as he will fail as he did when he tried to have Herod kill Jesus when he was born and Joseph and Mary fled to Egypt Matt 2:13-18.
During the battle of Armageddon Jerusalem will be captured and half the population will be taken into captivity and the other half will remain Zech 14:2

Zechariah tells that the women will be raped indicating that there will be genocide taking place because armies that rape also murder.
The half that goes into captivity indicates that some slave labour is required by the Gog and Magog nations. There would be a shortage of people at that stage in history because it will be the final days of the Great Tribulation and the world population will have been decimated under the rule of the Antichrist.
Some teachers say that this will be the time of Jacobs Trouble written Jerimiah chapter thirty but there seems to be a few problems with that idea.
Israel will be in captivity when they go through the time of Jacobs Trouble.
Jer 30:10 "My people, do not be afraid; people of Israel, do not be terrified. ***I will rescue you from that faraway land, from the land where you are prisoners.*** *You will come back home and live in peace; you will be secure, and no one will make you afraid.*
Over the years millions of Jews have returned to Israel to live; if they were afraid they would have stayed in the nation they came from. For example many American Jews have returned to live in their home land.
The worst time that the Jews have been living in other nations and suffered a catastrophic time of persecution was during WW2 and the Holocaust.
Seems that this chapter is referring to that event which was the greatest mass murder in history of a nation Two thirds of European Jews which numbered over nine million were murdered during WW2 which Zechariah

also prophesied in Zech 18:8. This is not to say that Armageddon will be any way an easy time for the Jews living Israel.

ANICHRIST DEFEAT

The defeat of the Antichrist will be similar to the destruction of Sodom and Gomorrah with fire coming out of heaven and destroying them Eze 38:21-23; however there will be a mixture of different outcomes against the Antichrist and his armies.

These invading soldiers will turn on and kill each other while others will be dying from some plague as well as fire raining out of heaven on them.

It does seem that it may be a prolonged war that is fought out over a period of some time. We see in Revelation nineteen when Jesus returns on His white horse and with the armies of heaven with him that are dressed in white robes that it is the sharp two edge sword that He will strike down the nations Rev 19:15. This indicates that Jesus will give these armies the opportunity to surrender and repent of their sins so long as they don't have the mark of the beast. Zech 14:16 says that that those who survived from those evil armies will go up every year to celebrate the feast of Tabernacles. It could be that the sharp two edge sword proceeding from Jesus mouth is also in the hands of those armies in heaven returning with Jesus and what they are doing is going out to preach repentance and salvation.

The armies that return with Jesus are the saints that have been raptured and attended the wedding feast because they are dressed in white which is the righteous act of the saints Eph 5:26-27, *Rev 19:7 Let us be glad and rejoice, and give honour to him: for the*

marriage of the Lamb is come, and his wife hath made herself ready.
Rev 19:8 And to her was granted that she should be arrayed in fine linen, clean and white: for the fine linen is the righteousness of saints.
Paul seems to confirm this in Two Thessalonians chapter two when he says that the Lord will destroy the Antichrist with the breath of His mouth and the splendour of His coming. This really does demonstrate the very nature of God that He doesn't want to destroy the world but rather save it.
Luk 9:55 But He turned and rebuked them, and said, "You do not know what manner of spirit you are of.
Luk 9:56 For the Son of Man did not come to destroy men's lives but to save them." And they went to another village.
Even at His second coming the Lord wants to reach out to the lost and it seems that the role of the armies with Him will be to fulfil this role.
For the ones that refuse to repent and have received the mark of the beast it will be a devastating defeat and there will be most likely millions that will die. Zech 14:12 tell us that their flesh will basically be cooked on their bodies while they are standing, but not all will die in this manner because the smell of rotting flesh will be so bad that people will be employed for seven months burying the rotting corpses these are most likely the ones that have died from the plague and of killing each other in confusion. The survivors of Israel will go out and gather the weapons and use that for power that will

last for seven years Eze 39:9. That is an incredible amount of oil that's been utilised from an invading army. The Lord says in Ezekiel thirty eight that they will cover the ground like a cloud.

MILLENNIUM REIGN OF CHRIST

The next event after the battle of Armageddon will be the one thousand year reign of Jesus from Jerusalem Israel.

It will be then that Satan will be locked up in the abyss Rev 20:1-2 for the Millennium reign of Jesus and the Antichrist and false prophet will be defeated and thrown into the Lake of Fire Rev19:20. The world will be free from evil spirits that tempt and deceive people into rebelling against God.

For Christians this event should the greatest news ever and should considered as a reality for what is coming. We are often excited about an up and coming holiday with anticipation of what to expect. This event should have us jumping for joy and watching and waiting in expectation.

It's difficult to understand why most of the evangelical and charismatic churches aren't all over this subject. There will be a day that the Lord restores the world to something like it was when the world was created Zech 14:6-9.

When the lord returns physically to earth then after he has defeated the Antichrist and False Prophet the world will be renewed starting at Jerusalem as living waters come out from the Temple in Jerusalem and form a river that will flow into the Dead Sea and turn it into fresh water and be alive with fish and fruit trees growing along its banks. Eze 47-112. The prophet describes the day the Lord returns as a different day and at the end of the day there will be light.

This may be the day when the creation is restored as the world will most likely be in a mess after the events of the Great Tribulation like waters turning into blood and heat and fires destroying much of the earth.
Isaiah the prophet gives us a clear insight to what will be coming into, this scripture speak so beautifully on its own.
Isa 65:17 "For behold, I create new heavens and a new earth; And the former shall not be remembered or come to mind.
Isa 65:18 But be glad and rejoice forever in what I create; For behold, I create Jerusalem as a rejoicing, And her people a joy.
Isa 65:19 I will rejoice in Jerusalem, And joy in My people; The voice of weeping shall no longer be heard in her, Nor the voice of crying.
Isa 65:20 "No more shall an infant from there live but a few days, Nor an old man who has not fulfilled his days; For the child shall die one hundred years old, But the sinner being one hundred years old shall be accursed.
Isa 65:21 They shall build houses and inhabit them; They shall plant vineyards and eat their fruit.
Isa 65:22 They shall not build and another inhabit; They shall not plant and another eat; For as the days of a tree, so shall be the days of My people, And My elect shall long enjoy the work of their hands. Isa 65:23 They shall not labor in vain, Nor bring forth children for trouble; For they shall be the descendants of the blessed of the LORD, And their offspring with them.

Isa 65:24 "It shall come to pass That before they call, I will answer; And while they are still speaking, I will hear. Isa 65:25 The wolf and the lamb shall feed together, The lion shall eat straw like the ox, And dust shall be the serpent's food. They shall not hurt nor destroy in all My holy mountain," Says the LORD.

IN SIMPLE LANGUAGE

Jesus made the point to the Pharisees that they should be able to read the signs of the times. He likened it to being able to forecast the weather by sky in the morning. In other words we should able to evaluate what national or global events will happen by the current trends.

A good example of this is what happened before WW2 when Hitler began his push through Europe in the late 1930s. Anyone who was a realist and paying attention saw the type of person he was and his extreme political policies knew that he was itching for war. The same can be said for Russia at the turn of the last century with the rise of communism and the Russian revolution.

The average Russian lived in poverty while corrupt leadership led a selfish and decadent lifestyle. Both of these movements were responsible for the murder of millions of people.

Then in the late 1980s the communism experiment failed completely and the Soviet Union collapsed into smaller nation states.

While the communist countries were disintegrating the west was beginning its freefall into moral breakdown that will eventually see its demise.

The crazy part about it is that the west will take on the communist ideology even after seeing its total failure. That gives an insight just how powerful the power of Satan is when Gods people turn away from the truth. What is even crazier is that this moral breakdown and move towards communism will move exponentially fast.

If you are taking notice you will observe that the faster our morals move away from our Biblical foundation so our politicians become more and more totalitarian. This will eventually lead to a total collapse of our society.
While we are in chaos because of corrupt government and our financial system crashes it will be then that China will invade and conquer us.
If people are paying attention and listening to what the enemies are saying you will understand that white Caucasians are going to be wiped of the planet in a genocide that will make the Jewish holocaust look a mild persecution.
We know this because they are using similar language that the Nazis were using about the Jews before the holocaust.
Once again we see the stupidity of the left in full display because they are the ones talking this poison and for the most part they are white Caucasians.
WW3 will cause such a huge disaster people will be desperate for some civil order to be put back in place and they will allow a one world government to rule over them with a very charismatic man leading.
It will be at this time that Jesus will take the people who belong to him to heaven for the wedding feast. There will be many Christians who will miss out on this event because they were not paying attention.
When they see that they have missed this great event they will be absolutely gutted and many will fall away and give up because of the difficult times the world is

experiencing and the fact that they missed out on the wedding.
The believers who do not give up will be on fire for God and preaching the Gospel worldwide with power and great miracles.
This will be the greatest move of God in history and everyone on the planet will have the opportunity to hear the Gospel.
When they have finished the task of preaching the Gospel to the whole world they will be attacked by the Antichrist and they will be killed and silenced. For the people who rejected their message will celebrate the fact that these believers who were causing such great havoc to the world have finally been silenced.
After this happens God's judgement will be released upon the earth like never before which is written in Revelation sixteen.
About this time the Antichrist will become enraged and set to destroy Israel with a huge army that consists of a coalition of nations like, Russia, Iran, Turkey, China and North Korea; this is what is called the Battle of Armageddon.
Seems that this battle will last for a little time and people that have joined that evil coalition will still have the opportunity repent and be saved so long as they have not received the mark of the beast 666. This clearly demonstrates God's compassion and mercy for His people.
After the Battle of Armageddon Jesus will begin His earthly reign of what is called the Millennium; this will

be a wonderful time where there is no evil spirits to deceive or oppress the world's population.

THE COMING BATTLE

With any war or battle that is fought there has to be a strategy or plan and spiritual warfare is no different. There are different reactions to different types of conflict, for example:

If an army patrol is ambushed soldiers are trained to act in certain ways so that they are not thrown into utter confusion which would result in annihilation. During training they will rehearse many different types of possible outcomes so that they will respond to confront the aggressor with minimum losses.

The gathering of intelligence is one of the most important aspects of a pre-battle preparation and that was demonstrated in the Battle of Midway in 1942 when the US navy sunk four Japanese aircraft carriers and turned the tide of the war.

It is important for the church to have good intelligence so that it can successfully wage war against the devil and defeat him.

The main weapon that the church has is prayer because it is then that God will respond if we ask, Luke 18:1-8. It was prayer that caused God to come down and visit Sodom in person as He said to Abraham that He would see if the situation was as bad as the cry that come before him was in Gen 18:20.

It was the prayers of the saints that moved God to have the seven angels blow their trumpets of judgment upon the earth.

Rev 8:3 And another angel came and stood at the altar, having a golden censer. And many incenses were given

*to him, so that he should offer it with the **prayers of all saints** on the golden altar before the throne.*
*Rev 8:4 And the smoke of the incense which came with the **prayers of the saints**, ascended up before God from the angel's hand.* If there was ever a time in history for the church to be active in warfare against Satan it is now as the church is becoming less and less relevant and weaker by the day.
The Bible is clear that we are the stronger and have the greater weapons as it says in 2 Cor 10:4 that our weapons are not carnal but mighty through God for pulling down strongholds. Also Paul tells us in Eph 6:12 to put on the full armour of God. That would mean living by the word of God rather than the doctrine of man and trusting in the Lord for everything.
The present situation cannot be allowed to go on unchecked by the church any longer; it's time to speak up and speak out with courage and then get down to some very serious and pointed prayers because the abuse of children will utterly destroy the next generation.
Now that we understand the legal issues that God is constrained by, and that He is bound to His own Law and He cannot and will not go against it.
It is up to the church to unite and send petitions and prayers to heaven to have Satan removed from his position as prosecuting council against people before God because Satan has legally overstepped his authority by the changing of human DNA and having laws administered to turn children into homosexuals. It will

be then that God will be able to order Michael and the armies of angels in heaven to have Satan and his angels thrown out of heaven down to earth Rev 12:7. And then Jesus will truly be Lord of Lords and King of Kings.
Rev 12:10 Then I heard a loud voice saying in heaven, "Now salvation, and strength, and the kingdom of our God, and the ***power of His Christ have come****, for the accuser of our brethren, who accused them before our God day and night, has been cast down.* It is up to the church to act first and then God will respond.
This will be one victory more to move us closer to the return of Jesus.

JESUS MUST BE GLORIFIED

When we consider all that the Lord has done for us it's now time to really glorify Him and the work that he is done. This will be a great step to getting ready as the bride dressed in white; the white is the righteous acts of the saints Rev 19:8.

We as a fallen people can never be perfect while we are still in this mortal body and so Jesus won't be coming back for perfect people because if that was so then we would never make it to heaven.

The only way we can be ready is as it says in Ephesians five twenty six that it will be by the washing of the word of God, not the doctrine of men.

That really is a pretty simple statement!

Follow what the Bible says that we live our lives and run our church meeting according to the Word of God.

1. Don't give ourselves a title like Pastor, Reverend, Bishop or teacher Matt 23:8.
2. Don't make covenants with governments Isa 30:1-3, Gen 14:22.
3. Teach, look and long for Jesus return Matt 24:45-46.
4. Call out government policy and defy if contrary to God's Word ACTs 5:29.
5. Preach hell and warn people of sin and its consequences Matt 5:22.
6. Build the church on the gifts of the Holy Spirit and the fiver fold ministry gifts 1 Cor 12:1-11 & Eph 4:11.If believers follow these simple directives then the bride of Christ will be dressed in white and ready with a lamp full of oil Matt25:1-13 for the return of Jesus.

These acts would truly glorify Jesus and give Him Lordship over His church rather than the king of Sodom and it will be then that the church can experience a great outpouring of the Holy Spirit with all signs wonders and miracles.
It will be then that Jesus will be glorified because when we have this mind set then we are totally dependent on Him and Him alone.
Imagine when a couple is about to get married and when the wedding day comes the bride is not dressed in her wedding gown and when they come to bring to the wedding she tells them that she wants to go shopping. The bridegroom would be devastated and upset and would most likely tell her that the wedding is off.
'I wonder what the bridegroom would do!
THE END

CPSIA information can be obtained
at www.ICGtesting.com
Printed in the USA
LVHW021433011222
734355LV00017B/1123

9 781470 994280